COACHING PERSPECTIVES V

Center for Coaching Certification

Cathy Liska

Laurissa Heller

Margi Bush

Clinton Ages

Ellen Zebrun

Jennifer Mount

Tim Dean

Michael Zaytsev

Renee van Heerden

Meg Hanrahan

Marie Snidow

Brian McReynolds

Julie Binter

Amy Gamblin

Dear Reader,

Each year talented individuals further expand their skills with coaching. Now, as certified coaches through the Center for Coaching Certification, these coaches are sharing their expertise for the benefit of fellow coaches and individuals alike.

The breadth and depth of knowledge, insights, and tips contained herein are a testament to both the intelligence and the compassion of each author. It is a privilege to work with them during their training and as they further their coaching work and careers.

Each chapter is easily readable independent from the others and the combination of all the chapters is worth reading for the full impact of the specific insights and tips.

Kindly let us know how we can be helpful.

Sincerely,

Cathy Liska
Guide from the Side®
Center for Coaching Certification

CENTER FOR COACHING CERTIFICATION

www.CenterforCoachingCertification.com

Info@CenterforCoachingCertification.com

800-350-1678

MISSION:

Enhance your coach training experience with
quality, professionalism, and support.

VISION:

A high-quality, ethical norm throughout the coaching
industry achieved through leadership by example.

For coaches,
those thinking about becoming a coach,
and those who receive coaching.

Table of Contents

Language is the Foundation *by Cathy Liska*………..…………..……….1

Building Rapport in Coaching *by Laurissa Heller*………………27

Responsible Risk Taking *by Margi Bush*………..………..…………48

Elevation Exceleration *by Clinton Ages*…………..……………..70

The Power of a Personal Brand *by Ellen Zebrun*……...................89

Accessing the Client Network *by Jennifer Mount*………..…......109

Coaching Millennials *by Tim Dean*…..129

Coaching for Dating Success *by Michael Zaytsev*……………..148

Choosing the Right Life Partner *by Renee van Heerden*………......171

Transition Coaching *by Meg Hanrahan*…………………..…......195

Vulnerability in Leadership *by Marie Snidow*…..……...............218

Coaching: The Art of Management *by Brian McReynolds*…..…...238

Coaching for Master Learners in Academia *by Julie Binter*........259

Career Coaching: Staying within the Lines *by Amy Gamblin*.....280

LANGUAGE IS THE FOUNDATION
Cathy Liska

Consider how language impacts you personally. Test it by thinking about something you want to accomplish. Say to yourself, "I wish I was able to do it." How does that feel? Now say to yourself, "I am moving forward and doing it." How is that different?

While the research behind language and positivity is extensive, it is mentioned only briefly here to invite your further exploration. This chapter is a story highlighting the personal and coaching perspective of language.

Positive language creates positive thinking which creates positive feelings that lead to positive actions which create positive outcomes that build confidence which supports positivity. Whew! Using positive language for exploring and acting on thoughts, feelings, and behavior is the foundation for maximizing success. A high level of positivity enhances brain capacity and function, and impacts confidence.

Language used to express thoughts and beliefs creates self-fulfilling prophecies. Reframing challenging or negative experiences with positive, proactive language supports positivity and confidence. Talking about wins and good experiences also

1

supports confidence and creates positivity, plus builds momentum. Positivity and confidence enhance individual ability to face challenge and change. Positivity through language enhances skills including decision making, proactivity, and emotional intelligence.

> *"Positivity through language enhances skills..."*

MEET TWO BROTHERS

Explore the impact and power of language through the lives of two equally talented brothers: Brendan is a talented athlete who excels in sports; Kevin is a natural musician who is skilled with several instruments. Both brothers are good students. Throughout this story, for each area of their lives, notice what happened, what was said, what they thought, and ultimately how language impacted them.

EXTERNAL VERSUS INTERNAL LANGUAGE

Brendan and Kevin played soccer during their middle and high school years. Brendan was a hotshot with the ball and scored most of the goals during games. Brendan was also a solo operator. Kevin was a team player and held the players together on the field, heading the defensive effort. Kevin was an unseen talent.

After a game, teammates told Brendan he did an awesome job and congratulated him on scoring goals. Brendan tended to dismiss what the other players said and instead thought, "I wish I had more support out there," or "Man I can't believe I missed that one goal" instead of hearing what was said. As a result of his internal, negative language focused only on himself, Brendan distanced himself from the team and saw himself as separate. Instead of feeling good about his achievements he got wrapped up in being frustrated.

Kevin's teammates talked as a group about how the team did well during the game. Comments to Kevin included "good game" as they left the soccer field. Kevin affirmed what others said in his own mind thinking, "We have a good team and I like being part of it," and "I feel like I added value." Kevin felt good about his contribution and felt good about being a part of the team.

The comments from their teammates were external to each of the brothers. How they thought about what was said and their own thoughts were internal.

> *"How they thought about what was said*
> *and their own thoughts were internal."*

3

COACHING NOTES

Ask your clients how they think and feel about what is happening and what they want to achieve. If their response is negative, ask how they want to think and feel. Work with them until they find their positive internal language. As a coach the skills of modeling and asking for positive language along with exploring internal motivation are significant in terms of value and impact for clients.

> *"...ask them how they want to think and feel."*

External motivation means doing something for someone else or to avoid a consequence. External motivation has a short term impact. Internal motivation means doing it because of the value personally. Internal motivation has a long term impact. The language used creates negative or positive motivation. Ask clients for their positive, internal motivation.

Hints for Your Research: In a Ted Talk Dan Pink speaks about the science behind intrinsic motivation. Neuro Linguistic Programming describes internal versus external Meta Programs or thought processes. Studies done by the universities of Illinois and Southern Mississippi state coaches are partners and provide the supportive environment for increased motivation. These university studies state that asking instead of telling makes a difference and this is the foundation of effective coaching.

4

WORD CHOICE MATTERS

Rejoin the two brothers now. Both did well in school. For Brendan the biggest challenge was accepting the authority of teachers and administration. Kevin wanted more of a challenge as he found school easy.

When Brendan's teachers gave instructions, he heard them tell him what to do and how to do it so he only partially listened. He was consistently reminded, "You should follow the instructions." The more he was given direction, the more Brendan repeated to himself, "I hate being told." Each time he was told, Brendan mumbled to himself, "I can figure it out myself." The teachers thought he was somewhat rebellious and considered it typical of boys. The more Brendan became frustrated the more the teachers told him what to do, which in turn reinforced his negative thinking. Brendan distanced himself from authority figures.

Kevin was reminded by teachers to focus more or that, "It comes easily to you so it is important you apply yourself to complete it." While Kevin realized that it was important to apply himself, he thought to himself, "I am smart and I want more of a challenge." Over time Kevin began to find ways to challenge himself. He timed his reading and worked ahead in the math book to see if he could figure it out on his own before having it explained.

5

During class, he paid attention to how the teacher explained it to find differences from what he had thought. He learned to challenge himself.

The way he was told fostered resentment in Brendan and his irritation grew. Kevin heard supportive language. He learned acceptance for circumstances, acknowledged his own abilities internally, and developed a habit of challenging himself to learn and grow.

Word choice influences how what is said is understood and processed. Some words limit and other words empower. While most of us are unaware most of the time of limiting words, the impact remains.

> *"Word choice influences how what is said is understood and processed."*

COACHING NOTES

Focus on the future in coaching sessions. If a client is giving the negative story or focusing on what they don't want, ask questions to create the shift to focus on the positive and what they do want. As a coach, model positive, proactive language. Ask questions so that clients use positive, proactive language. The positive language supports positive thinking which in turn supports success.

It is unfortunate that it is easier to flow with the negative and critical. When the focus is positive, supported by positive language, brain function improves and people achieve more.

> *"When the focus is positive, supported by positive language, brain function improves and people achieve more."*

Hints for Your Research: A number of books explore how words influence conversations, thinking, and outcomes including those by Luntz, Cialdini, Newberg, and Waldman to name a few. Dr. Emoto experimented with the impact of words on water that was then frozen. Caples studied persuasive writing extensively. Bobbins blogged on how many negative words there are in the English language. Neuro Linguistic Programming provides a body of knowledge on the impact of words. Canfield shared research on how humans process more than twice the amount of negative as compared to positive. There is an old saying that garbage in is garbage out and the garbage is the negative.

WORDS INFLUENCE INTERNAL THINKING

Back to the brothers: both played musical instruments. Brendan was a decent saxophone player. Kevin was extremely talented with the violin and clarinet. Brendan did enough to get by and was mostly interested in opportunities to be a show-off. Kevin was invested in the music and wanted to advance

7

with higher-level instruction; advanced training was unavailable.

Brendan's teacher said, "You are pretty good at it but you could do better." Brendan thought, "Yeah, sure, but… so what, this is all right for now and I just don't care."

To Kevin the teacher said "You really have a talent." Classmates told him, "I wish I could play like that!" Kevin thought, "Well, I am going to enjoy it because I am good at it plus I really dig this music."

Over time Brendan's disinterest grew and as soon as he completed his required classes he stopped playing music. Kevin did as well as possible with what was available and had fun with it.

When the teacher said "but" Brendan dismissed the first part of the statement and focused on the remainder. He decided he didn't care if he could do better and it wasn't worth it. Kevin felt good about his skill and focused on enjoying the music.

COACHING NOTES

"Be very intentional with word choice and model language that conveys confidence and is positive."

Be very intentional with word choice and model language that conveys confidence and is positive. Ask clients to commit to their goals instead of a maybe or hesitating by using doubtful words. This means instead of saying might or possibly, say, "You are good and you are improving," expressing positive support and belief in future possibilities.

Hints for Your Research: Experiments and research by Dr. Lipton show that the energy of positive or negative thoughts is one of the controls of our biology. Newberg and Waldman, in Words Can Change Your Brain, say that a single word influences physical and emotional stress.

LONG-TERM OUTCOMES FROM THINKING HABITS

Fast-forward to the working world of Brendan and Kevin. They both work at a car dealership. Brendan is in car sales and he does well. He is a persuasive and has a talent for closing tough deals. Kevin handles the financing for customers. Brendan had fun for a while and then lost interest because the work seemed repetitive. Kevin found there were limitations on financing options for customers.

The sales manager, to motivate Brendan, said things like, "Keep going man, you should try and get back on track! Go sell

9

another one!" Brendan thought to himself, "Yeah, I guess I should try… oh well, I sell enough."

Customers told Kevin, "Thanks for your help." Kevin felt good about helping and shared with his manager, "I really want to help people." Kevin asked, "Will you support me in researching resources I can refer people to as an alternative when I can't help them?" His manager said "Absolutely. Run what you come up with past me first." Kevin went on to say, "I want to streamline the process." His manager said, "If you can figure out a more efficient way to do it I will recommend a bonus for you!"

Brendan continued with decent sales numbers, enough to get him by on his earnings and maintain his position. His job was just a job. Kevin found ways to improve the process. He also found options for helping customers qualify to buy a car. Kevin built a reputation for helping people and earned more customers for the dealership.

COACHING NOTES

Ask clients for possibilities. Ask questions in a way that invites clients to express their possibilities confidently, believe in their opportunities, and confidently commit to their goals.

Model confident language and ask questions so that clients list possibilities with positive, confident words. Confidence is a way of thinking. Confident thinking is the foundation on which positivity effectively builds success. When clients think confidently and positively they are confident, happy, and achieve more.

> *"Model confident language and ask questions so that clients list possibilities with positive, confident words."*

Hints for Your Research: Research on confidence and positivity is available in Psycho-Cybernetics and The Benefits of Frequent Positive Affect. Confident thinking is based on confident language which supports healthy self-esteem.

POSITIVE VERSUS NEGATIVE

Move now to the personal lives of the brothers and reflect on how their thoughts over time influence their feelings and behaviors now. Brendan was a popular party guy with lots of girlfriends. Kevin was the stable one with a solid marriage and a nice group of friends. Brendan shied away from commitment because he focused on short-term gratification and playing hard. Kevin thought about the positive side and was happy so he felt good about his life.

11

Brendan's friends said, "Ah let's just forget work and go have a good time." The girls he dated asked, "What is your hang-up with commitment?" Brendan thought to himself, "Yeah, I'm just having a good time. Why settle down? I have my freedom instead." When Brendan got the flu, he stayed home alone. Overall Brendan felt restless.

Kevin's friends commented on his marriage saying, "You are really a lucky guy." His wife told him, "I am glad you are in my life." Kevin thought to himself, "I am very fortunate." Then Kevin was diagnosed with cancer. People said to him, "Wow, I guess the good do die young." Kevin chose to stay with his positive focus and said to himself, "I have lots of support." He talked openly with his wife about the diagnosis. His friends helped him research treatments. Kevin's doctor answered his questions and worked with him on the treatment plan. Kevin's friends helped him and his wife through the process. Kevin is now cancer free and feels the whole experience was a blessing because he is stronger. Kevin learned to be aware of his priorities and learned how much his friends really cared.

COACHING NOTES

"Focus on opportunities, possibilities, and the positive, proactive approach to making it happen."

Focus on opportunities, possibilities, and the positive, proactive approach to making it happen. Consider that Return on Investment or ROI studies on coaching often cite qualitative benefits that include improved relationships and increased confidence. In each coaching session use language that reinforces the positive with confidence. For example instead of saying, "What might you do?" ask, "What will you do?"

Hints for Your Research: Harvard Business Review provides research that instead of success providing happiness, happiness creates success. A number of studies look at the benefits of positivity on health and wellness. Ultimately, being positive improves opportunities.

LANGUAGE AND FOCUS FOR CREATING MEANINGFUL CHANGE

The car dealership where Brendan and Kevin worked became increasingly proactive in employee development. They offered training and started a coaching program. Brendan was resistant. Kevin signed up for coaching.

In the initial conversation Kevin's coach Rachael asked Kevin what he knew about coaching. Kevin was hesitant and said he knew very little. He cited experience with his soccer coach. Rachael asked Kevin what he gained from the time with his

13

soccer coach. Kevin thought a moment and expressed his appreciation for the coach's patience and guidance. Rachael gave Kevin time to add to his thoughts. He said his coach gave him good directions.

Rachael explained how coaching in athletics with the giving of direction is different than professional coaching. She shared that coaching is designed to support Kevin finding his own positive direction and developing his own game plans. Kevin asked, "What if I don't know the answer?" Rachael explained that there are coaching techniques to discover the answer within and that as his coach she partners with him in the process.

As Rachael and Kevin worked together they started by exploring his big picture interests, influencing factors, motivation, and priorities. In addition to addressing work place goals Kevin was given space to address personal goals. This supported his increased focus at work.

Because of his new awareness through coaching Kevin prioritized things he wanted to change in his life. For example he started conversations with his wife about their future. It meant that instead of going along with what happened they became proactive about creating their ideal path. Together they made changes at home so they felt their life was relaxed and at the same time purposeful.

At work Kevin wanted to figure out how to add value and make a difference. Rachael asked Kevin to describe what he did now and what options he wanted to create. During the exploration Kevin realized that he wanted to approach his boss with alternatives for prospective customers that failed to qualify for financing. He wanted to help them and help the company too. As a result Kevin created a program for helping customers unable to obtain financing buy a car through alternative financing. This meant he helped the dealership increase sales, customers gain reliable transportation, and the financing institution to both serve the underserved and earn a profit in the process.

Kevin was very happy with what he changed and accomplished through coaching. His family was happy too. Kevin's boss and company were happy with his initiative and how the dealership sold more cars while also helping underserved individuals.

COACHING NOTES

> *"Coaching conversations are focused positively because they are about what a client wants to accomplish."*

Ask the client what they want to achieve. Coaching conversations are focused positively because they are about what a client wants to accomplish. Support this with positive, confident language. Ask questions to find the internal motivators expressed positively that support long-term success.

Hints for Your Research: At a Science of Coaching conference brain scans showed the increase of brain activity with positivity. Cited research showed positivity creates chemical changes. Studies demonstrate the exponential difference of positive, internal motivation.

COACHING THE CHALLENGING CLIENT

Brendan was aware that Kevin was making changes, saw improvements in his already good family life, and experienced the impact of Kevin's initiative at work. After a year of observing this, Brendan decided to consider coaching.

Brendan met with Rachael and liked her approach. He was worried about Rachael coaching him since she also coached his brother. Rachael explained confidentiality in coaching per the International Coach Federation Code of Ethics. Brendan also wanted to be clear with Rachael that he was his own person. Together they talked through how coaching really supports exactly that. Brendan decided to go ahead with a few test sessions to see if it was going to work. Rachael explained that

16

because coaching is a process and creating change takes time, she wanted Brendan to commit to six sessions before starting. After hesitating Brendan decided to commit.

In the initial session as Rachael asked Brendan about what he wanted in all different areas of his life, she observed that Brendan focused on getting away from what he did not want instead of moving toward what he did want. Each time Rachael then asked Brendan to describe what he wanted instead. Brendan was challenged to focus on what he was moving toward. He was unclear on how answering Rachael's questions made a difference until he became aware of an internal shift in his own thinking to be more positive and proactive. Initially after the coaching sessions Brendan stayed with his habits and routines. He forgot about the change in focus and how it felt different.

> *"...he became aware of an internal shift in his own thinking to be more positive and proactive."*

In a subsequent coaching session Rachael asked Brendan how his thinking impacted his outcomes. She asked how his thoughts became a barrier. Brendan realized that when he looked at half a glass of water he saw it as half empty instead of half full. He reflected out loud with his coach. As the coaching sessions continued Brendan explored whether his perspective made a difference in his outcomes and realized that it was influencing him without his being aware.

17

As Brendan began shifting to thinking about what he wanted and how to make it happen, he said things to his coach that she challenged. For example, when he said he should do something, she asked if he wanted to do it. Brendan pushed back and asked, "What difference does it make?" Rachael invited Brendan to say the same thing several different ways and reflect on the difference for himself. For example:

- I should be more positive with customers.
- I want to be positive with customers.
- I choose to be positive with customers.
- I plan to be positive with customers.
- I will be positive with customers.

Rachael asked Brendan to express his buy-in to being positive with customers for each of the different ways of saying it. Brendan realized that saying he wanted to felt like he had control and was more engaged. Saying he should felt like someone else was pushing him and he resisted it. Saying will was a commitment and it meant it was time to figure out how to do it. Brendan discovered his words made a difference in his thinking, feeling, and doing.

At the end of their fifth coaching session Rachael asked Brendan what he was gaining through coaching. Brendan talked about his awareness of the difference between his habit of being negative or pessimistic and this new way of thinking positively and being proactive. He stated that he learned his word choice directly impacted how he perceived things, thought about things, and ultimately behaved. By choosing language that gave him internal direction and control plus focusing on the positive and being proactive, he moved from feeling stuck or trapped to realizing he had options. He became aware that ultimately it was his choice to stay where he was and blame circumstances or do something different. Rachael congratulated Brendan on his progress and success with this awareness and invited him to give himself credit and a pat on the back.

> *"By choosing language that gave him internal direction and control plus focusing on the positive and being proactive, he moved from feeling stuck or trapped to realizing he had options."*

Rachael asked Brendan if he wanted the sixth session of his commitment to be his last or to continue. Brendan chose to continue coaching. Brendan said he wanted to review his goals in all areas again and then prioritize.

Brendan's sixth coaching session was powerful. Each time Rachael asked a question Brendan challenged himself to answer in terms of what he wanted. By the end of the conversation he felt that his life was in a good place and he had very real opportunities and choices. In their next session Brendan focused on choosing priorities. He decided to work on his personal life in terms of being open to a long term relationship. He decided to work on his career by fully engaging and challenging himself to be the top sales person each month.

During the coaching process Brendan explored what and how to change. He decided he wanted to relax when he went out and really engage in conversations. Brendan went to the same places with the same people and actually paid attention to them. He slowed his pace. Brendan's friends knew something was different and at the same time were unable to put their finger on exactly what. Women that Brendan talked with responded to his attention with interest in really communicating. Some became great friends. During his coaching sessions Brendan reflected on what happened and realized that he was being respectful of others. He felt good and his relationships were authentic. As this became his new norm Brendan began developing a strong, long-term relationship.

Brendan decided that he was going to apply what he was learning in coaching about being positive and proactive with words that supported that focus in his work. He asked customers what they wanted in a car and what that did for them. He asked them about their process for getting a car. Customers became more comfortable working with Brendan. In addition to closing sales at a higher rate, Brendan began building a referral network. His customers sent others they knew and told

20

them to ask for Brendan. Brendan met his sales goals and succeeded in his challenge to himself to be top sales person.

Rachael congratulated Brendan on his progress and success. She then asked him how he wanted to acknowledge himself. Brendan realized that by giving himself credit he felt confident and that in turn helped him to succeed.

Then Rachael asked Brendan what else he wanted. For a moment Brendan was stunned. He realized that by changing his thinking to be positive and proactive, then changing his language to support that, he had achieved his goals. Now he had the opportunity to expand his thinking and set new goals.

> *"He realized that by changing his thinking to be positive and proactive, then changing his language to support that, he had achieved his goals."*

Brendan continued working with his coach and building on his success. He began training other sales people on how to work with their customers.

COACHING NOTES

Reflect, research, experiment, test, and observe impact using affirmations, stories, meditation, journaling, and visualization.

More than reading information that is available, practice the techniques because when you experience it yourself you know the power and impact.

Hints for Your Research: Read the research on how positive affirmations are a tool for supporting a positive way of thinking and belief. Visualizing the desired outcome is tool used by many including professional athletes. Stories invite interest and positive stories create positive emotions for positive engagement. The research ranging from studies to experiments to brain scans backs up the benefits of being positive. Being positive means both thinking and speaking positive language.

HOW TO CREATE CHANGE

Start by asking yourself these questions about what you want:
- What does saying it like that mean?
- How does it feel?
- What do you want to focus on?
- How do you want to feel?
- Which words hurt?
- Which words are positive and proactive?
- Which words support your success?
- How will you create a habit of positive thinking and talking?

Reflect on your answers. Some do this through journaling, others through planned time for reflection, and others with their own coach. Decide for yourself what works and how to apply the insight. Create your positive, proactive plan and create a habit of using language that supports your success.

Start with creating your own positive, proactive focus with a habit of using language that supports you and others.

Limiting Language	What to Say Instead
Try	Choose to
Need	Want to
Should	Will
Would	Plan to
Could	Commit to
Can't	Doing
Won't	Prefer to
Don't	Instead do...

COACHING NOTES

Ask the client for their positive, proactive language. Ask the client what language works for them, what words they want to use, and how they will create a habit of positive, proactive thinking to support them for the long term.

As the brothers experienced throughout their lives, negative language limits thinking and outcomes while positive language expands thinking and enhances outcomes.

> **"...negative language limits thinking and outcomes while positive language expands thinking and enhances outcomes."**

 Cathy Liska is founder and CEO of the Center for Coaching Certification and the Center for Coaching Solutions. As the Guide from the Side®, she is recognized among the best in training, coaching, conflict management, and consulting. Cathy has trained and facilitated thousands of events, workshops, certification courses, and organizational retreats.

Cathy has earned the following designations: Certified Master Coach Trainer, Certified Master Coach, Certified Consumer Credit Counselor, Real Estate Broker, Certified Apartment Manager, Certified Family Mediator, Certified Civil Mediator, Certificate of Excellence in Nonprofit Leadership and Management, Certification in the Drucker Self-Assessment Tool, Grief Support Group Facilitator, and Certified Trainer/Facilitator.

Her three coaching niche areas include Business Development, Communication and Conflict, and Intentional Choices. Cathy balances training other coaches, coaching up to 12 individual clients at a time, writing, publishing, and volunteering.

Cathy's personal mission statement is "People". Focused on empowering others, Cathy is known for her passion to support others achieving the results they desire.

www.CenterforCoachingCertification.com

BUILDING RAPPORT IN COACHING

Laurissa Heller

What exactly is rapport and how does it show up in coaching? Rapport is an understanding between two people. It is developed through shared knowledge, language, and experiences. In coaching, what a client conveys in terms of values and culture are precious threads for engaging them as an individual. This shared energy and information, filled with personal vitality and world view, are the supporting roots of a client. These foundational gems are collected through focused listening and reflecting back, ensuring and demonstrating that a client is heard and acknowledged. While this action is a simple transfer of correspondence between two people, it builds trust and is a base from which to grow a relationship.

> *"These foundational gems are collected through focused listening and reflecting back, ensuring and demonstrating that a client is heard and acknowledged."*

Some relationships gel immediately due to backgrounds or familiar cultural experiences, and other times the foundation is built through how coaching sessions are managed by the coach. Understanding a new client begins from the very first introduction. From the first moment a client comes into contact, it benefits a coach to ask about them and what is most

27

important now. Ask a returning client too because values and motivation change over time.

Rapport is the number one indicator of success in coaching. When a client feels seen and heard, it melts barriers and brings about an expansive, meaningful direction. There are many key elements to coaching and with rapport client disclosure goes below the surface.

RAPPORT WITH NEW CLIENTS

People make decisions based on emotion, knowledge, and motivation. During the introduction process rapport building assists in landing new clients. As a coach asks about a client's goals, it is helpful to match their desires with what you offer as a coach. Thus the line of communication becomes personal. The client feels understood, supporting the success of the coaching relationship.

After signing an agreement, the next step is to begin the process of an in-depth inventory focused on what the client wants in all areas of their life and at this point in life. Coaches use various tools to learn about each amazing part of a client. For example, the broad focus areas for coaching are personal, relationship, financial, career, health, and lifestyle interests. The focus for executive, career, or business clients may be more work oriented; the whole person including their health and personal life is part of the equation. When going through the process of discernment around what a client desires and prefers, values show up in the conversation as well. So while many of these gems show up in the opening session or even through a values directed activity, often viewpoints and priorities are conveyed by a client through their explanation of daily life.

> *"When going through the process of discernment around what a client desires and prefers, values show up in the conversation as well."*

MEET AL

While I was growing up my mother had a friend who helped us with stuff around the house. From changing the oil in my car to vacationing in Canada, he was ready to assist. He had his own photography business, owned huskies, built engines, wrote proposals, climbed mountains, worked for NASA as a contractor, and the list goes on. Whatever he dreamed, he pursued with a full heart. He was a renaissance man. Let's call him Al.

As a child, I wondered how he made friends everywhere we went together. How was it that Al became such a vital person

29

in each situation or conversation?   How did he make the most unlikely people his buddy?   It was the same with whoever he encountered.

> *"How did he make the most unlikely people his buddy?"*

One time we were locked out of our car after a hike in the woods.   With nobody around for miles, it looked like we were going to have to hike at least another 10 miles to a phone.   We were already tired from hiking half of the day.   We wanted water and food.   While it was getting to be dusk with only trees and birds to be seen we were deciding upon our plan of action.   By the way, this was before cell phones.   As we started to walk, motorcycle guys with leather jackets rode into our part of the park.   Al, who was a scientist at heart, and looked every bit of it, walked over to them after they parked their bikes.   I held my breath.   He talked to one of them for a bit.   The guy was 6'4 maybe, with a beard, an oddly shaped helmet, and a gang logo on his jacket.   We watched as Al engaged yet another new friend.   Soon after the exchange between them the motorcycle guy came over with a tool and worked to open our door.

Sure enough, the guy opened our car door.   I don't know how it was that the biker had that distinct tool on that very day.   Maybe he helped people on a regular basis?   All I know is that

30

on that particular evening Al asked him to help us and he did. We were incredibly grateful for his act of kindness.

After we were in the car driving home, I asked Al what he talked to the biker about before he came over to open the car door. Let's call the biker Ray. "Oh," he said, "I used to have a motorcycle and I asked him about his bike, where he was from, and the places he liked to go. One of Ray's favorite things to do on his bike is to go watch the leaves change in West Virginia." Al knew his name, what type of bike the guy had, where he liked to go on his bike, and what his plans were for his next big ride. Al then said, "I then told him about a place which doesn't cost a lot that I like to stay in when I go to West Virginia."

Al was genuinely interested in Ray and wanted to know about him. Even after Ray opened the car door, Al was chatting up a storm with him. He had built rapport with this biker who he just met.

> *"Al was genuinely interested in Ray*
> *and wanted to know about him."*

While Al was not coaching, the rapport he developed was based on how people respond to open questions concerning who they are in life. When there is genuine interest without judgment, humans open up. Even when someone comes from a vastly different experience, finding interesting things about each person allows for a more meaningful exchange. The highlight here is that Al loved to learn about people. He looked for the experiences he could relate to and constructed questions for each person with whom he was speaking. It didn't matter how someone looked. For example, he found knowledge that bonded him with his new biker friend. It seemed that Ray the biker felt seen and esteemed by their conversation too.

Some people have the natural gift of rapport with most every person they meet. Al was one of them. While a coach looks for these threads of connection with each client, sometimes it takes an effort to build.

The skills listed here are competency areas to assist with the building of rapport in a coaching relationship. How these skills are applied is as important as the skills themselves, meaning the tone and timing.

- Focused listening
- Common knowledge
- Common language and culture
- Understanding what a client wants
- Hearing and identifying values
- Understanding without judgment
- Authentic unconditional support

32

- Acknowledgements and encouragement
- Rephrasing the positive
- Self-Introspection (tend to your internal process as a coach)

Connecting through detached compassion with authenticity and staying on the question side of problem solving provides an open place for conversation. This is the doorway to unlimited creativity.

What follows is a deeper exploration of each of these skills.

FOCUSED LISTENING

Listening for values and traits of a client calls for a coach maintaining attentive listening over a period of time. While information and documents are exchanged as part of getting to know a client in a new relationship, often it is what a client doesn't see that floats into a coaching conversation to bring awareness. Tone, timing, cadence, and the delivery of verbiage from a client all contribute to a person's intentional communication. Like bread crumbs dropped along a trail for

"Listening for values and traits of a client calls for a coach maintaining attentive listening over a period of time."

tracking your way, people reveal values through the telling of a life experience or future desire.

Quality listening comes from being present. This is when a coach is so concentrated on listening that words are heard and also the energy is noticed from the inner experience of a client. The client sends out information while the coach collects it with the intention of directly reflecting it back to create clarity plus awareness of possibilities for advancement. The relationship exchange becomes a third energy and this is a vast window through which amazing discoveries take place. As believed in Chinese medicine, when two people come together the equal sum of their parts is much greater than two. It is infinite.

Body language is intentionally left off of the list of focused listening due to the fact that most often coaching is done over the phone and also it is more often misinterpreted than understood correctly. This leaves listening as a central skill for tracking a story. It means that hearing words and sounds becomes a vital resource for information. While many take it for granted or even think they are a good listener, it is a skill that is honed over years.

> *"While many take it for granted or even think*
> *they are a good listener,*
> *it is a skill that is honed over years."*

COMMON KNOWLEDGE BETWEEN CLIENT AND COACH

Connecting through means of common information or experience is what often brings a client to a coach. People hire a coach because of a subject matter area expertise, life experience, and perspective. Maybe the coach is extremely likable; what is it about the coach that creates that feeling for a client? Something is resonating. The common knowledge is a point of connection. Credentials and employment background show up most prominently during the hiring stages of coaching. The bottom line being that people want to know that a coach understands who they are now. Of course ultimately the power of the coaching is that the client finds their own expertise within.

While commonality and work background do assist with powerful questions and understanding, coaching skill is built with the 11 Core Competencies from the International Coach Federation to create openings and new viewpoints, eventually leading to successful goals. What clients are seeking is rapport. It is a coach's job to find common ground for the purpose of being an asset and at the same time begin the process of developing rapport.

While work or life experiences assist with the initial conversation, there are additional ways to create rapport in a coaching relationship. For example, before our first phone conversation, one client of mine who is an executive at a tech company did not see me as her potential coach because she thought she should work with someone who had executive experience. Then, after discussing what she wanted in life and work, it was clear that I had what she was seeking because of my background in families. During our initial call, she talked about the role that her family was playing in her work and how she wanted to pursue life. It became clear that my coaching experience fit her overall ideals. Sometimes it takes a conversation to learn where the crossover exists.

> *"Sometimes it takes a conversation to learn where the crossover exists."*

LANGUAGE AND CULTURE

It is clear that a common language is key when it comes to making inroads with cultural and national variances of people. Tones and sounds have the potential to change the meaning of words depending upon culture. One example is the Spanish language; there are at least four dialects of Spanish. As another example the English language transforms within the U.S borders from North to South. My Pennsylvania cousins are keen on the words yous guys. The change in language is even more pronounced when jumping over the pond as the Brits like to say.

Jumping over the pond means crossing the Atlantic. Language modification continuously transforms our vocabulary. For instance, in the U.S. short hair on the forehead is called bangs and in England it is called fringes. There are islands in the Chesapeake Bay area where the decedents from John Smith speak Old English and have many terms for the word blue crab. The Eskimos or Inuits have many variations or words for snow; it is debated just how many there are, anywhere from 50 to over 100 terms. The meaning changes with slight tone inflections.

"The meaning changes with slight tone inflections."

Precise vocabulary is warranted for particular life situations as part of employment or life experiences as well. For example, a caretaker of an ADHD child has specific language terms and so does an executive of a technology company. These are just two examples of the diverse language areas within coaching. Social media is another whole environment which has impacted language considerations too.

Clients show up in as many ways as there are people in the world and what each one is looking for in a coach is a sense of understanding about who they are along with a recognition of what goes on in their daily life. Of course, clients want a sense of support for their ambitions too.

When there is a gap in understanding do make the effort to learn the client's language. Seek to find meaning in their words and vision. Build questions from there.

> **"Seek to find meaning in their words and vision.**
> **Build questions from there."**

HEARING AND IDENTIFYING VALUES

Values are so essential to rapport that the word has been showing up throughout this chapter. Hearing what a client says about something that is important to their lifestyle and manner of living is tied to values.

In coaching there has been some confusion from clients about what exactly a value is and what it means. In this day and age, the word is often associated in the context of religion or politics and this does play a role for some folks. The word value encompasses a much greater circumference of meaning. Values are ideals that one believes about how to live and work, and are used to create priorities in life. These building block pieces of information connect a coach to a client's perspective in all aspects of life. Choices about eating, sleeping, health, relationships, money, family, education, material possessions, and whatever else are based on values. Awareness of this is an

38

asset to living purposefully with joy. Each person holds their own vision for how this looks.

When a value is heard, it is helpful to reflect this back to a client. It brings clarity for decision making. It reinforces what is important and puts ideas in a framework which at some point will lead to action. There is often ambiguity around what is going on in a client's life, creating fog between how time is being spent and what is actually a personal value. Organizing which ideals belong to a client and what is connected to the surrounding environment assists with self-awareness and decision making. Matching values with goals is a home run.

The reconnection of action with values brings a client into congruency. This act in itself builds a strong bridge for future potential both for success around goals and additionally for the coaching bond.

UNDERSTANDING WHAT A CLIENT WANTS

The process of reflecting desires back to a client is in itself empowering. Rephrased words and verbiage often sounds different coming in through the ears as opposed to going out of the mouth. Furthermore, open ended questions unlock expanding possibilities in a client's mind. This simple measure

39

has the potential to bring awareness to a client in a very powerful way. Both of these skills build the relationship between two people, enhancing the rapport in a profound manner.

There are countless open questions which move a client into forward thinking. How a client speaks and in turn hears their desires through the rephrasing from a coach is sometimes an ah-ha moment. The ironic response when a client hears their words rephrased, "Wow, I've never heard it that way before," makes it real. This takes it to a new level of engagement. It is a very empowering experience for a client.

> *"How a client speaks and in turn hears their desires through the rephrasing from a coach is sometimes an ah-ha moment."*

UNDERSTANDING WITHOUT JUDGMENT

As the client discusses goals the coach tracks the story. The coach is seeking to understand exactly how and where a client is at now and in moving forward through their life. Meeting each individual without preconceived notions creates the space for the client to express them self freely. Sometimes there is a gap between how the client explains a situation and how a coach hears it. It takes diligence to check as a coach, to know if you

40

as the coach have an internal web the story is caught up in as part of your personal views. Coaches keeping their personal values separate from the coaching session interactions will encourage clients to dig deeper.

As long as the thoughts expressed in the exchange are within the ethical boundaries of the competencies, it is all about how the client sees the situation. First seek to understand, collect client information, and when it is appropriate challenge negativity and shine light on ambiguity.

AUTHENTIC UNCONDITIONAL SUPPORT

Authenticity gives a coaching relationship quality and thus builds upon rapport. The unconditional support comes from a skill of emotional detachment from the decision making of a client. This gives the client the ability to be their empowered self, directing their own choices, which is the point of this coaching work.

There are times when a client steers away from initial goals. It is up to the coach to ask how newly discovered goals fit with the original purpose of the relationship and also of the client. What are the reasons for the change? What is their perspective now? A coach may challenge a client in this situation, with

41

continued support for the decisions made by the client. The rapport built creates an environment for the challenge to be well received. Additionally, the authenticity strengthens the relationship bond.

ACKNOWLEDGEMENTS AND ENCOURAGEMENT

Acknowledgement and encouragement are potent elixirs for clients. Both lift people up emotionally and give them a sense of confidence. Encouragement through new territory enhances communication with positive energy. Furthermore, it assists people with linking to the world of possibility. Positivity generates an environment where dendrites and axons have an opportunity to connect with other dendrites and axons which then gives neurons a road to travel toward action. Positive language is that powerful. Our brains have the potential to change. As clients move in a positive direction, their brains make new roads for positive action. This both lifts the client and it additionally makes the bond of the coach and client stronger.

> *"Positivity generates an environment where dendrites and axons have an opportunity to connect with other dendrites and axons which then gives neurons a road to travel toward action."*

REPHRASING THE POSITIVE

Rephrasing shows up throughout this list of skills because it affirms ideas and assists with action oriented thinking. By paraphrasing positive words, thoughts, and actions of a client, a coach produces a growth environment. This also lends itself to neuroplasticity, the rewiring of the brain. Once a pathway of success is formed the ability for action increases.

Each positive thought is a stepping stone for the next. The greater the amount of effort a client invests in positive verbiage the more that client will gain from the coaching session. It really is that simple. Rephrasing is an excellent tool to keep people on the exciting, joyful parts of their venture. It also highlights the positive within the relationship, which again reinforces the bond.

SELF-AWARENESS WITHIN THE COACH

Internal rapport sets a tone for what one is able to extend into the relationship. For the coach, recognizing and managing what is going on within around thoughts and emotions when in a coaching session is an advanced skill. This means being in touch with how words and situations affect personal views while still focusing on the client. Creating an open space for the

43

client by managing personal opinions keeps the stream of communication flowing between the coach and client, thus building a deeper comfort level. Keeping personal views in check takes a continuous internal radar.

Another part of this is maintaining wellness as a coach. Personal wellness enhances a coach's ability to coach effectively. Wellness is defined by each coach who seeks to stay congruent with their own set of values. For some this may mean eating a well-balanced diet. For others it may mean going to church, walking outside, visiting with friends, meditating, or maybe it is quiet time in the garden. Whatever brings a sense of harmony assists with tuning each coach like a guitar over time. While the sound and communication of the instrument are enhanced, there is also a process of listening to an internal sounding board.

> *"Personal wellness enhances a coach's ability to coach effectively."*

Furthermore, it is of assistance to be connected to other coaches to learn, exchange ideas, and continue the process of expanding understanding of communication within the boundaries of coaching. This builds a professional community sounding board with which to reflect upon coaching competencies.

CONCLUSION

All of these skills contribute to rapport within a coaching relationship. This in turn rewards clients with the growth benefits sought after as part of the reason for hiring a coach. In fact, all of these coaching skills overlap and interconnect, weaving a beautiful tapestry of exchange. Sometimes it comes naturally and flows freely and other times it takes a little more consideration to find the common areas of understanding.

The bottom line is that when bringing on a new client it is incumbent on the coach to consider how each new situation has the potential to grow. It is the job of a coach to create a safe and inviting place for each client. Reflecting upon common knowledge or vocabulary benefits the communication. Listen without judgment and rephrase with the intention of positive possibility. A supportive environment carries the client in a space of forward motion.

Laurissa Heller is a Certified Master Coach, a Trainer, and a Mentor Coach. She is an Associate Certified Coach through the International Coach Federation. She assists clients from across the globe with personal growth opportunities. Whether it is coming up with a plan, working through ambiguity, or setting a new course she enjoys learning about each client's vision for life. She has an innate ability of assimilating vast information into simple communication for a client's review.

Laurissa earned a Master of Science degree in Health Promotion, and has served as an adjunct professor with Maryland University's Integrated Health coaching program. Her experience in education, non-profit leadership, project management, and teacher training assists her with a diverse background for understanding of each amazing client.

Laurissa lives in Maryland with her three teens who keep her young through life's adventures. She volunteers with Stand Beside Them, a pro bono program that provides veterans with coaching. "Living your dream," describes exactly how she feels about her coaching career.

Laurissa@CenterforCoachingCertification.com

Finding Space for Responsible Risk Taking
Margi Bush

Generally speaking, risk is defined as the probability of loss which could cause someone or something to experience an unpleasant result. Professional and personal growth requires that the client to push out of their comfort zone and into a responsible risk-taking zone. It may feel scary and uncomfortable. In the risk-taking zone the client will create opportunities to gain courage, strength, and confidence by expanding possibility.

How will Decision Making Change if Risk Taking is a Good Thing?

Responsible risk taking can bear fruit; it is often difficult to get a client to come out of their comfort zone long enough to shake the fullest trees and gather the juiciest bits. What causes this resistance? In my experience it's been the fear of failing. As a professional coach, I have found clients are often satisfied with the low hanging fruit or even fruit found on the ground. Call it fear, acceptance of mediocrity, or longtime personal and comfortable habit. Coaching your clients to take responsible risks can support them running for a ladder, climbing to the top of the tree, and discovering the quality they truly want.

Consequently, once they ease into responsible risk taking they become aware of the benefits of setting their sights on the higher quality yield for ultimate success.

Life can be difficult and a lot of work. It is also a journey of adventure, education, and the unavoidable act of taking different forms of responsible risk. Our personal attitudes, inner-monologues, pre-conceived notions, learned responses, and variety of life experiences (and those of our clients), most likely color our thoughts about risk taking. We're warned at various stages in life to play it safe. Can this warning sometimes take us off track? Do we allow this fear of failure, this imagined safety net, to keep us unproductive and separated from our goals?

> *"Our personal attitudes, inner-monologues, pre-conceived notions, learned responses, and variety of life experiences ... color our thoughts about risk taking."*

As coaches, how far do we push a client toward goal achievement? What if it involves quick and decisive action or, ultimately, responsible risk taking? Change begins with awareness of where we are versus where we want to be and then assessing the responsible risks we are willing and able to take along the way. Professional coaches can be the traveling companions of choice moving with the clients toward the results they want. We have the distinct ability to assist the client in defining and enhancing their agenda while setting and accomplishing designated goals. This is often facilitated by responsible risk taking.

At the beginning of the coach/client relationship we enter into an agreement with the client listing and clarifying the coach's and the client's roles. Ideally we are also discussing the possibility of responsible risk taking to achieve the intended goals. Keeping the client's goal in sight, both verbally and in written form, will encourage them to take action steps in logical, doable increments. This will repeatedly address the client's fear. The coach will explore concrete evidence that the direction is worthwhile and help the client to recognize small victories along the way that assist the client in finding the courage to get through the stress involved.

History is full of stories about people such as inventors, entrepreneurs, and military figures who took responsible risks to accomplish their dreams and goals in order to move forward successfully. For example, Charles Darwin presented new evidence concerning the theory of evolution by natural selection that was contrary to traditional thoughts. Paul Revere rode in the middle of the night to carry the news to militant leaders about the advancement of British troops at great risk if he was unsuccessful. Abraham Lincoln is an example of a leader who took calculated risks. When he won the presidency, he named individuals from the opposing party to his cabinet. What are the reasons he gave his political enemies such power? Lincoln reframed responsible risk taking and recognized they would help him see the other side of future political issues. These individuals frequently dealt with other people's perceptions and expectations which were often alien to their own. Imagine if they had given up when faced with the fear of responsible risk taking. They often referenced difficult times as being the inspiration for later achievement of goals and dreams. Where did these responsible risk takers find their strength and courage? Perhaps their measure of the importance associated with the risk changed or their courage may have begun to outweigh the risk of failure. The appearance of risk is an interesting concept and somewhat subjective. What may appear as a risk to one client may not be a risk at all to another. How do we move our clients beyond their particular self-limiting fear of failure to explore responsible risk taking? Keeping the big picture in mind and the client's goals in sight will help achieve small victories.

> *"Keeping the big picture in mind and the client's goals in sight will help achieve small victories."*

These successful milestones along the way will act as motivational tools to maintain the client's focus and serve as a positive reminder of the stated goals.

EVALUATE GOALS BASED ON THE SPECIFIC

The client may come to you with an inability to relate to well-known risk takers. They probably see their own risk on a totally different scale from that of a famous example they may know. The challenge for a coach is keeping the client fully present and aware of the importance of articulating where they are and where they want to be using their own scale of abilities. Successfully supporting the client as they move from their comfort zone into their risk-taking zone demands flexibility from the coach. The following example that I am sure many are familiar with may leverage your performance as a coach to effectively support clients. It illustrates the coach's role in the client risk taking process and the possible transformation that may follow.

Many of us have taught our children or someone else to ride a bicycle. This is a significant milestone that is accomplished in one's early life. Once learned, it opens up the perceived world to the individual. Finally, achieving that skill parallels with the responsible risk taking five step process.

Initially beginning with training wheels (the coach) and slowly raising them to the point of maintaining balance independently is a trial and error process. Once the balance is learned, we as parents or the coach run with the bicycle to prevent a fall. In

52

the end the learner rides faster than the coach can run so is now on his or her own power.

A coach recognizes and remains supportive during the client's moments of responsible risk taking as they struggle. Watching the client accomplish the hard work while also continuing to clarify their intentions is challenging. Our task as coaches is to remain supportive in their discovery of their ability to do the work and achieve the goals they want. A coach creates a safe space and facilitates an environment for the client stepping out of his or her personal comfort zone. Thus the client accomplishes what he or she wants and what they possibly regarded as impossible before the coach / client relationship.

> *"A coach creates a safe space and*
> *facilitates an environment for the*
> *client stepping out of his or her personal comfort zone."*

QUESTIONS TO EXPLORE CLIENT RISK-TAKING READINESS

The questions for determining readiness to take responsible risks will improve the client's comfort level with the process.

1. What does responsible risk taking mean for you?
2. How do you approach responsible risk taking?
3. How do you manage responsible risk taking in your life?

4. What do you want?

5. Name a responsible risk you have taken.

6. What helped you build confidence when taking responsible risks in the past?

7. What resources do you have for support?

STEPS IN THE RESPONSIBLE RISK TAKING PROCESS

Our comfort zone can be described as a place where we feel safe, at ease, and in control. A place where we choose our actions because we focus on the outcome we want. The following risk taking process provides a guide to move clients to thoughtful action. It empowers them to see risk taking as a path for growth and achieving what they want.

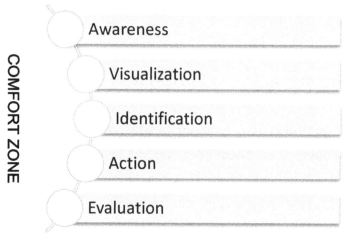

Awareness: It is beneficial that the clients have a keen awareness of where they are in their journey, knowledge of their strengths, and of their challenges. Self-awareness may feel different at first and as a coach you help the client anticipate the differences and recognize their desire to make changes. Some clients may come from a place where they are comfortable with creating and implementing change and others are more cautious as change brings about uncomfortable feelings. Helping the client increase his or her awareness will support their awareness of where he or she wants to go and how to get there. Working with a coach, the client will consider the risks and then calculate and strategize. The coach is their partner for wandering into new territory. Their inner monologue can be very persuasive at times and may prevent them from responsible risk taking. A coach will assist the client in taking a deep dive using self-awareness exercises. Powerful questions such as the ones suggested below help manage a client's inner critic and encourage more positive self-talk.

Visualization: Visualization can be a powerful activity when a coach co-creates scenarios where a client explores certain situations. He or she can experience taking action from a safe perspective, supporting their ability to visualize his or her true potential. By helping the clients connect with their desires at this deep level they are significantly more connected to the things they want to accomplish. Through visualization they are preparing to be present and grounded when it's time to act on their desires. It's important to recognize that helping the client discover what they want is a first step. Visualization can help them with how they will actually do it. Powerful, open-ended questions are key in visualization and goal setting.

> *"It's important to recognize that helping the client discover what they want is a first step."*

QUESTIONS FOR AWARENESS AND VISUALIZATION

1. What do you want your future to look like?
2. What do you like about where you are now?
3. What do you want?
4. What are your passions?
5. What are you doing to live your passions?
6. What are your values?
7. What are you doing to live your values?
8. What do you want to change?
9. What are your possible outcomes?
10. What will your outcomes feel like?
11. What will you see?
12. What will you hear?
13. What resources do you have for support?
14. What resources do you want?
15. What will happen if you take some responsible risks?

Identification: The coach's role is supporting the client during responsible risk taking by asking them to list action steps for achieving their goals and then set a timeline for accomplishing each action. Clients will learn how to change their way of doing things so they achieve new and successful results. Open-ended questions are important in guiding the client with establishing action steps and timeline.

"Clients will learn how to change their way of doing things so they achieve new and successful results."

QUESTIONS FOR IDENTIFICATION
1. How do you want to move forward?
2. What behaviors or habits do you want to change or acquire?
3. How will you take care of yourself while working on your actions steps?
4. Describe how responsible risk taking will get you where you want to be.

Action: This is the part of the process where clients take action. They are changing behaviors and feeling uncomfortable because they have moved into the risk taking zone. You may observe clients experiencing the imposter syndrome. (Imposter syndrome is when people are in a position that comes with generally perceived competence while at the same time questioning their own competence.) The client may feel anxiety as they move through the risk taking process. Be aware of the potential of feelings of chronic self-doubt as clients push through their comfort zones into responsible risk taking and continue to move them forward. A Circle of Responsible Risk exercise follows. It is a useful tool for clarifying the client's priorities for action, assessing progress, and holding clients accountable for stated goals.

The Circle of Responsible Risk is a tool to fulfill our purpose in keeping the client's goals in mind as they choose what they want to achieve and then create action steps. The Circle of Responsible Risk is a coaching tool that supports a client as they customize their wedges and identify their level of success in areas of their life they want to change.   The eight wedges of the circle represent different areas in the client's life they identify as areas that are creating a difference between where they are presently and where they want to be in the future.   The Circle of Responsible Risk exercise empowers a client to stay the course they choose and visibly see their progress.

After the client answers the questions in the awareness, visualization, and action steps of the risk-taking process, the client will identify eight key areas in which they want to change. On the Circle of Responsible Risk, the client will place a value between 1 (very dissatisfied) and 10 (very satisfied) in each area reflecting his or her current level of satisfaction. Then the client shades portions of each wedge in proportion to that number from the inside to the outer edge. When shading is completed, the client will have visual clarity of their current level of satisfaction in each area they choose in the wedges of the wheel.

Next, the client completes a second Circle of Responsible Risk exercise and this time places a value between 1 (very dissatisfied) and 10 (very satisfied) in each area reflecting the level of satisfaction the client wants in the future. Both exercises provide visual clarity for responsible risk taking and later goal setting.

When each Circle of Responsible Risk exercise has been completed, the client will chose a few areas as a starting point where they most want to improve and then begin goal setting. The open-ended questions below may be used after completion of present and future Circle of Responsible Risk exercises to assist the client in creating action steps for achieving what they want moving forward.

"... the client will chose a few areas as a starting point where they most want to improve and then begin goal setting."

CIRCLE OF RESPONSIBLE RISK EXERCISE

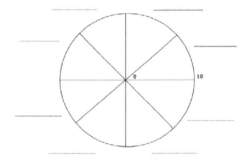

Questions for Taking Action

1. What will you do?
2. When will you take each action?
3. How will your action steps push and stretch you?
4. Describe your life after the changes you make.
5. How do your action steps align with your purpose?
6. How do your action steps align with your values?
7. How do you want to be held accountable?
8. How do you want me to support you?

Evaluation: at this step in the process, the client will have completed two circles: one for present level of satisfaction and a second for the wanted level of satisfaction. The Circle of Responsible Risk exercises give the client a picture of their identified areas for taking responsible risk, the specific steps to achieve their goals, and timelines for completion of each goal.

The client sets the timelines. Responsible risk taking is a continuous loop and calls for consistent evaluation on the part of the client to determine where to make course adjustments. As coaches, we see and take time for celebrating the client's successful milestones. This will help the client rise above the details of their action steps and see the big picture, which is brighter than they realize.

Questions for Evaluation
1. What are your outcomes?
2. What did you learn?
3. What do you want to do differently?
4. What are your next steps?
5. How do you want to celebrate your successes?

IMPLEMENTATION OF RESPONSIBLE RISK TAKING

"Clients come to us because
they want to create change in their lives."

Clients come to us because they want to create change in their lives. Helping them see results and working from their agenda moves the client forward and supports them as they come out of their comfort zones. Competent coaching is accepting the client where they are when they come to us, responding to the client's wants in the present, and guiding them toward the future according to their agenda.

Co-creating a coaching relationship with the client begins with asking what the client wants and determining what a successful coaching relationship looks like to them. Asking the client open-ended questions that clarify what they want to achieve through the coaching process helps the coach consider what models and tools to draw upon to meet the client's objectives.

Unconditional acceptance of the client helps the coach develop good rapport with the client and create a process where they can share openly. Unfortunately we often learn along the way in life that acceptance is conditional which means that we learn we have to be at our best to be liked and accepted. Working with the client demonstrating a non-judgmental approach helps move them past assumptions from their past experiences.

Two key skills for coaches to display are active listening and rephrasing, which demonstrate that a coach cares about the client and cares about their success. This builds trust with the client and provide opportunities for the client to move past self-limiting beliefs. It supports the client in their walk to the edge of responsible risk taking and then to take a positive leap toward future goals. Active listening is critical in the coaching relationship and is demonstrated by maintaining good eye contact and displaying relaxed and approachable body language. Rephrasing techniques empower a coach to check for understanding of what the client has said plus develops trust and rapport with the client.

Success is a path we choose to take. Remember it is a journey that includes many components along the way. Powerful open-ended questions can take the client to new places and challenge them to feel comfortable being uncomfortable while making changes. Open-ended questioning allows the client the ability to build his or her own resourcefulness. Ask the clients, what does your mind's eye picture of success look like?

The five-step risk taking process and the Circle of Responsible Risk empowers the coach to approach the coaching relationship with a clearly defined framework and simple tool so the client can better focus on what they want. Working through the five-step process and the Circle of Responsible Risk helps you as coach to make keen observations and consequently ask appropriate, powerful questions moving the client toward future focused clarity, goal setting, and successful goal achievement.

Entering the professional coaching business has greatly changed my own definition of success from an external focus to an internal one. As a coach my primary focus is on assisting the client in structuring his or her own pathway to success. The coach also acts as a catalyst to ease them into considering responsible risk taking as a component of that journey. Responsible risk taking is one variable that was previously missing in their formula for success.

> *"The coach also acts as a catalyst*
> *to ease them into considering responsible risk taking*
> *as a component of that journey."*

The Circle of Responsible Risk exercise will help a client better respond while in the space between stimulus and response then move them past where they are currently to where they want to be. The concrete example that follows illustrates the power of the Circle of Responsible Risk exercise in working with a client I will call Anna.

CASE STUDY: RESPONSIBLE RISK TAKING WITH ANNA

Anna was a successful VP of Human Resources in a large multi-state organization. She had everything she had dreamed about: a fancy title, an office with a window overlooking a beautiful, newly renovated downtown street, and a nice salary. She was dissatisfied. She longed for something more in alignment with her values. The organization she worked for had grown significantly in the past three years and Anna saw the organization losing sight of its mission and values. Because the business had expanded Anna was working longer hours late into evenings and often on weekends. She believed she had enough experience and training to start an HR consulting business. Owning her own business meant an opportunity to be aligned with her values, purpose, and passion. Anna hired me as a coach because she lacked the confidence to leave the organization and start her own firm.

After answering the questions in the awareness, visualization, and action steps of the risk-taking process, Anna identified eight key areas (four personal areas on the left side and four professional areas on the right side of the circle) in which she believed her level of satisfaction was low. Each wedge of the circle represented areas Anna identified for her goal of having her own business. Anna and I explored what responsible risk taking meant to her and how leaving her comfort zone moved her forward toward her goals. Anna placed a value between 1 (very dissatisfied) and 10 (very satisfied) in each area reflecting her current level of satisfaction. She then shaded in each area from the inside to the outer edge. When shading was completed, Anna had clarity of her current level of satisfaction.

Next, Anna completed a second Circle of Responsible Risk and this time she placed a value between 1 (very dissatisfied) and 10 (very satisfied) in each area reflecting the level she wanted to be in the future. This exercise gave Anna more clarity for responsible risk taking and for her later goal setting. When each Circle of Responsible Risk exercise had been completed Anna chose two areas as her starting point, what she wanted most to improve. Then she began goal setting.

Each session with Anna gave her the opportunity to examine and rethink her approach by considering things from a different vantage point. The Circle of Responsible Risk guided Anna in achieving her action steps. Paying attention to Anna's responses to the questions I asked provoked deeper inquiry and discovery of what was most pressing to Anna in the moment.

Anna left her job as the VP of Human Resources and began a small HR consulting firm eight months after our first coaching session. The five-step process and the Wheel of Responsible Risk Taking exercises provided Anna with tools, giving her a substantial push to do what she thought possible.

CHALLENGES AND REWARDS

In working with a client, pushback, deflecting, or outright denial sometimes happens. The coach may find it appropriate to ask the client about moving himself or herself, even temporarily,

66

from their comfort zone and insert themselves into the possibility of taking a risk. In order to achieve goals inserting a certain degree of responsible risk taking will propel them towards the goal or make the reasons they have not yet reached it apparent to them. The general consensus of risk taking is dealing with the probability of loss or having something negative happen as a result. The connotation of risk often involves fear and trepidation and these are challenging aspects.

The coaching process is a future-oriented process and requires a shared commitment on the part of the coach and the client. The coach demonstrates confidence and strong coaching presence. Adequate preparation at the beginning of the coaching relationship will consist of the coaching agreement and review of coaching ethics. The coaching relationship is structured around the client's agenda. Coach will find the five-step responsible risk process and the Circle of Responsible Risk exercise useful guides in maintaining structure during discussions around setting and achieving a client's goals.

> *"The coaching process is a future-oriented process and requires a shared commitment on the part of the coach and the client."*

Rewards are the outcome of responsible risk taking.

Margi Bush, SPHR, CMC is President of Collaborative Thinking LLC, a Charleston, WV based human resource partner for individuals and businesses. Margi focuses on leadership development programs, performance management, and employee engagement. She serves on the Board of Directors for the Charleston Chapter of Society of Human Resource Management as their chapter President and is VP of Programs and Events for the Association for Talent Development (ATD) WV Chapter. She is a member of the International Coach Federation (ICF) and the ICF Charlotte Charter Chapter. She is a graduate of Leadership Kanawha Valley and Leadership West Virginia.

Margi is a Certified Master Coach offering one-on-one coaching, team coaching, and leadership coaching. She is an accountability partner acting as a catalyst for change which provides the client an opportunity to focus on what they want. Margi's open-ended questions, genuine curiosity, and active listening helps her clients in being the captain of their own ship, fostering self-awareness, helping her clients develop resourcefulness for creating and sustaining the purposeful life that they want. Margi is a Certified MBTI® Practitioner and she is qualified to administer the FIRO-B instrument.

www.collaborativethinkingwv.com

ELEVATION EXCELERATION

Clinton Ages

Throughout the history of time, humankind has aspired to be the best and greatest performer in any arena, whether kingdom, sport, tournament, product sales, or business size. High performance has been rewarded by society and has been prominently coveted by multiple members of society. In many of the examples of our celebration of the high performing hero, we acknowledge the supporting role of the individual assigned to keep the hero focused. This individual is, perhaps, the less celebrated coach tasked with supporting the hero's performance. The coaching role, although easily overlooked, is the most important person in the hero's rise to greatness.

When thinking about the concept of coaching, the focus is around the usefulness of the practice in developing people's skills and abilities, and working towards improving performance and accomplishing aspirations. Successful professional coaching is framed in a program designed to methodically assist an individual with achieving their specified goals. This is true whether the individual's intentions are oriented in their executive capacity, growing a business, or their personal career development. It applies when their intentions are rooted in their personal management of life and relationships or in their pursuit of wellness. The purpose of coaching is for the coach to partner with their client, also known as the coachee, to boost their effectiveness and performance and help them work towards embracing their full life's potential. I even expand this concept to encompass equipping the coachee with the skills to develop their own processes for continuing to be successful.

I devised my own coaching program that is founded on the basic principles of coaching, business analysis, and project management. I call it Elevation Exceleration, an abstraction of the coaching philosophy with a unique underpinning factor. This unique factor is defined with a combination of words: the word Elevation, and the two words Excel and Acceleration concatenated into one unique word which I have fashioned, Exceleration. The phrase is formulated from a few basic concepts, which tied together, construct a dynamic that embodies and enhances the coaching perspective and is representative of my personal philosophy. The goal of the program is to increase capacity for accomplishment, facilitating development of a rhythmic cycle of accomplishment, simply meaning that the more you get done the better you get at getting things done.

By definition, elevation means to raise status to a higher reference point. It indicates that the subject of reference is above others in station and position. The word excel is defined as performing extremely well, better than average and reaching

71

superlative output.   Finally, the word acceleration is defined as the change in the rate of motion greater than the current displacement amount.   I translate this into a perspective which is in alignment with coaching, to mean that it is the sustained increase in the ability to accomplish identified tasks.

Leveraging the best practices found in Business Analysis and Project Management for defining and implementing technology solutions, I crafted Elevation Exceleration to be a coaching program designed to assist an individual's desire to improve personal performance at a pace which is faster than that which they are directly capable of achieving on their own.   The program is grounded in three pillars: 1. Motivation Affirmation, 2. Personal Energy, and 3. Relentless Self-Development.

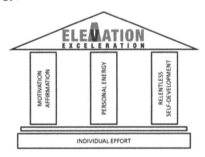

The first pillar, Motivation Affirmation, is the use of the power associated with positive words to inspire and invoke self-motivation.   It is a very familiar concept within self-help coaching, spirituality, and religion, placing emphasis on an individual generating change in their life through word selection and positive thinking.

The second pillar, Personal Energy, is the focus on linking together both the mental and physical aspects of a person and redirecting this combined energy positively towards the future. The idea of unity between the body and mind is based in historic philosophy; I theorize that this unification is an important source of personal power to be tapped into and used to fuel a person's motivational aspirations.

The third pillar, Relentless Self-Development, is the thought that an individual persistently seeking ways to improve them self centers on the importance of self-learning. With a single-minded endeavor to learn and develop self as a pillar, the expansion of knowledge facilitates heightened accomplishment. Thus, all three pillars are key components in supporting and sustaining individual growth and are soundly associated to the ideology of Elevation Exceleration.

MOTIVATION AFFIRMATION

Start now to expound upon the first pillar, Motivation Affirmation. It is a simple concept which obtains its power from the combination of two words juxtaposed to create a single notion. This notion conceives that affirmation is essential in motivation. It is sustained from the thought that all real world achievement flows from belief in the possibility that things can happen and that those things are manifested through the action taken to make them happen. Simply restated, an individual must believe that they can accomplish a task and make an effort to actually complete it. Motivation Affirmation is a metaphysical conviction that positive words spoken over a situation will produce the truth being sought, bringing those things into causality and existence.

When an individual speaks positive words, that person feels self-confidence over the seemingly challenging tasks all of us face. Then action is taken with a predetermined belief in success and the result is accomplishment in part or in total.

> *"When an individual speaks positive words,*
> *that person feels self-confidence*
> *over the seemingly challenging tasks all of us face."*

The concept of Motivation Affirmation exists in Christianity and in other religions as well. In Christianity, it is illustrated through the story of creation where the universe and the earth were spoken into existence. There are also many instances of miracles of healing and restoration where spoken positive affirmations and belief were the vehicle for victory over the challenge seen in the tangible world. In every instance, the spoken word coupled with intense belief caused the manifestation of the desired outcome.

Through Motivation Affirmation, I believe that every dream and every desire on which you wish to act begins within We look inside of ourselves, see our own potential, and then vocalize it. I have personally witnessed this concept in my own life as well as in the lives of my clients.

> *"We look inside of ourselves, see our own potential, and then vocalize it."*

One such client sought to craft a brand for her upcoming television show. The first action we took was to conduct a comprehensive interview to document all of her goals and to understand her own self-view. Next, I interviewed a defined list of people who knew her best in varying capacities, some as a colleague, some a mentor, others a manager, and others still as a client, as well as through several social settings. The purpose of interviewing these people was to obtain external views of my client and to compare those views with her self-view.

After finishing the interviews, a thematic analysis of the conversation results and my client's own words produced the naturally viable brand for her television show. Initially, a problem arose in the discussion of this information. My client had a hard time accepting the feedback given by her selected influence group (which was overwhelmingly positive in nature). She found it difficult to receive the words and praise expressed to shape her self-image.

She and I reviewed my findings with another pass of detail. Still seeking to be convinced, I asked her permission to proceed with sharing the proposed brand with her leadership team and she agreed. It was after her most trusted advisors cosigned the brand that she then began to slowly accept it as truth.

In an effort to move past the remaining remnants of reluctance, combining her words with the themes from the interviews I drafted several affirmation statements. Her assignment was simple: place the affirmation statements on her bathroom mirror, on her night stand, in her car, and keep a copy in her laptop bag. She was instructed to recite the statements four times a day, during her morning routine, at lunch, upon arriving home from work, and before bed, and to recite the affirmations four times each recital for thirty days. The result was a transformation in her thinking and her eventual belief in the statements, empowering her to live the brand which was developed, therefore propelling her television show. This created a brand which connected with viewers and garnered her an incredibly successful start.

Through this exercise it was evident that when life and energy flow throughout your being an unstoppable force is created. This is the basis for your ability to achieve. It was further demonstrated that when you open your mind to dream the wonders of the world become your possibilities.

76

Through Motivation Affirmation it is demonstrated that it is important for you to believe in yourself because your inner confidence empowers great possibilities and opportunities, therefore furthering your drive for completing your goals. What you focus on expands and shows up in your beliefs. Your thoughts give you immense power in the world. When you learn to leverage the power of your own thoughts, your life can change dramatically.

PERSONAL ENERGY

Personal Energy is the practice of synchronizing the mind and body. It ties together the aspects of mental energy and physical energy to produce a force, which when directed towards the future serves as a propellant for sustaining drive and momentum. This personal power and energy, when sustained and tapped into, will fuel a person's motivational aspirations.

So the natural question which comes to mind is the following: What are the steps to be taken to achieve this level of energy?

The answer is simple and involves very basic components; the first is understanding and adhering to the fundamentals of nutrition, meditation, and physical activity. There is lots of scientific evidence which reinforces the importance of eating

77

healthy foods, taking mental downtime, and maintaining a physically active lifestyle. Simply put, your body and mind communicate and this affects you physically, mentally, and emotionally. Respecting the relationship between your body and mind by strengthening it is the best way to enhance your natural endurance and propel your ability to get things accomplished.

> *"Simply put, your body and mind communicate and this affects you physically, mentally, and emotionally."*

My recommendation is to consider learning about tropology, also called food combining, as well as becoming aware of the discipline of eating according to your blood type as a path to nutritious health. I also suggest incorporating the practice of meditation into your life such that you are taking the time to disengage from the hustle and bustle of your everyday activities so that you re-center your energy and focus your mind. Lastly, activity in which you engage that involves some physical exertion is beneficial to your body and an important component of increasing the stamina to sustain your pursuit of your identified goals.

I personally encourage the combination of the use of tropology and blood type eating as a nutritional plan and health attitude. Broadly, tropology, or food combining, is simply being aware that your body digests some of the foods that you eat differently than others. With this mindset, you eat foods that complement each other during the digestive process and avoid combining foods which will cause digestive conflict. At the most simple level, the suggestion is to forgo eating meat proteins with starches and to incorporate lots of raw vegetables into your meal plan. I also recommend augmenting this by eating foods which best agree with your blood type. Each person has different nutritional requirements and there are guides for choosing the foods that will promote increased energy and in general help lead a longer and healthier life.

An excellent combination for providing your body with efficient nutrition is to engage in the practice of meditation. Meditation comes in many forms; one I practice and strongly endorse is the practice of yoga. Yoga is an excellent form of meditation because it also incorporates fairly rigorous physical activity. During your yoga practice, you are taught to channel your mental energy into your body and actually encouraged to seek the synchronization of your mind and your body. Because yoga can be a strenuous activity, meditation in its simplest form is merely taking time to disengage from daily life and rest your mind from thinking. Easy methods for meditation include taking the time to take a walk and clear your mind. I also advocate frequent time away from home in what I have coined the Power Sabbatical.

The Power Sabbatical, like a power nap, is a quick reset versus the hard shutdown (months away from work) associated with a traditional sabbatical. The Power Sabbatical process is to take one of the minor holidays your employer offers and to add a day to either side of it for a four day weekend. If you have dedicated all of your holiday time to family, then the alternative is to find a Friday, any Friday, and take it off for an extended weekend. I advise that you schedule your departure for Thursday evening and return home Sunday afternoon. Your entire time away is best unstructured, with the primary objective being to rest, slow your brain down, and open your mind to freely ponder your life and the things you wish to improve.

In addition to nutrition and meditation, it is important to include some type of physical activity in your weekly routine. Notice that the emphasis is physical activity as compared to exercise. As a down grade from exercise, physical activity involves taking extra effort to exert energy by use of your large muscles and your gross motor skills. This is specifically accomplished by performing continuous tasks like walking, running, swimming, roller-skating, or cycling. Merely taking the stairs at work instead of the elevator or walking to or during lunch are simple ways to add physical activity into your daily life.

The more physical activity you incorporate into your daily life the better you will feel physically. Moreover, coupled with a healthy and nutritious meal plan and periodic meditation, you will develop the energy levels to supply your drive towards accomplishing more in your life.

RELENTLESS SELF-DEVELOPMENT

As a society we've come to expect all of our gadgets, like cell phones, cars, TVs, and other electronic devices, to improve each year. We have the same expectations for our software, the websites we visit, and the countless apps we have downloaded on our cell phones. Even products like basketball shoes have new models which are introduced to the market annually. We are constantly inundated with the next release and the new and improved version of most things that we see in the market. With all of this focus on enhancement, I pose this question: What are you doing to improve your personal skills or your life in general?

> *"What are you doing to improve your personal skills or your life in general?"*

Corporations offering consumer products typically have a roadmap for improving the features of their products, outlining all of the details about the betterments to be made and the timeline for making them available to the public. Consumer demand and competition causes corporations and the products they deliver to enter into a cycle of continuous refinement and enhancement through a spirit of relentless upgrading, a spirit which when transferred to the application of a person converts into an attitude of relentless self-development.

Consequently, mimic the practices of corporations, meaning have a mission statement, a brand, a marketing strategy, a differentiated product offering, and a roadmap for improving. After all, we are our own product. This concept at it's best represents the upgrade paths used by commercial products. As the owner of your own product, it is important to have a vision for your upgrade and a path to revision.

There is a popular anonymous quote about success being tied to continuous learning. As continual learners, we act as a conduit of our energy which we use for making positive personal impact. Our driving goal as achievers in a highly productive society is becoming a consistently high performer. We strive to operate in this capacity. We share countless stories of human achievement and personal triumph and we encourage students, beginning as early as elementary school, to set lofty goals and seek to accomplish them. In my opinion, although we place emphasis on accomplishment, I feel that we have room to improve how we teach students the processes to help them complete all of the goals they set for themselves.

Once the mantra of relentless self-development is adopted, use a framework for becoming more systematic in your approach for accomplishing your goals. This framework supports managing your efforts and aids your ability to track your progress. As you strive towards upgrading and growing your product, a Personal Improvement Roadmap is a tool of choice for managing your process.

Like the product roadmap developed as a result of business analysis and used by corporations, the Personal Improvement Roadmap serves as the mechanism for organizing your upgrade path activities. Documenting your Personal Improvement Roadmap consists of the following steps:

1. **Time Box Your Accomplishment Period:** Give yourself an appropriate amount of time for accomplishing your goals. Typical time boxes for accomplishing personal goals are annual time periods (twelve months) and quarterly periods (three months).

2. **Identify Your Goals:** After determining your time box, identify which goals you desire to undertake during that period. I recommend attempting up to three goals at a time.

3. **Set Milestones for Your Goals:** Plan your goals with the steps and tasks you deem appropriate to get those goals finished. Assign completion dates to the tasks most important for the achievement of each goal.

4. **Map Your Goals and Milestones to Your Personal Improvement Roadmap:** Start by designating categories for grouping goals together. Then it helps to color code labels for each goal type category. Design a chart for visually mapping the color coded goals to the timeline and for tracking your progress.

Under the Relentless Self-Development doctrine, you are the champion and manager of your Upgrade to You 2.0, you are constantly seeking ways to expand your whole-self. The potential areas of revision are expanded beyond your professional persona to also embody goals related to your physical activity, creativity, hobbies, and career.

> *"... you are the champion and manager of your Upgrade to You 2.0."*

FINISH

The focus of coaching is to methodically develop people's skills and abilities. Coaching supports an individual's efforts in working towards improving their performance, accomplishing their aspirations, and achieving their specified goals.

As a program founded on the principles of coaching and software development management, Elevation Exceleration is the notion of looking towards the future. It is the effect of

84

accomplishment and the contribution to developing momentum. I believe that the more you get done, the better you get at getting things done. This increases your confidence. The better you get at getting things done, the more you increase your capacity for accomplishment. You then develop a rhythmic cycle of accomplishment.

Elevation Exceleration is designed to bolster an individual's ability to improve personal performance at a pace which is faster than that which they are directly capable of achieving on their own. It is a partnership between the coach and client to boost effectiveness and performance and help you work towards embracing your full life's potential and equipping you with the skills to develop your own processes for continuing success in accomplishment.

It all begins with Motivation Affirmation and the use of positive words to inspire and invoke self-motivating life change through word selection and positive thinking. Success is amplified through your Personal Energy by linking together both your mental and physical selves and then redirecting your combined energy positively towards the future. Your attitude of Relentless Self-Development centers on the importance of self-learning and the persistent seeking of ways to improve yourself.

The combination of the three pillars, Motivation Affirmation,

Personal Energy, and Relentless Self-Development are key components in supporting and sustaining individual growth and developing your rhythmic cycle of accomplishment.

> **"The combination of the three pillars,**
> **Motivation Affirmation, Personal Energy,**
> **and Relentless Self-Development are key components**
> **in supporting and sustaining individual growth and**
> **developing your rhythmic cycle of accomplishment."**

Clinton Ages is a Strategic Technologist, Certified Professional Coach, Certified Scaled Agile Framework Program Consultant, and a Business Architect/Process Engineer with over 15 years of experience in technical solutions development, technology, and management consulting.

He has a Bachelor of Business Administration degree in Computer Information Systems, a Master of Science in Management of Technology from Georgia Institute of Technology, and is pursuing a Doctorate in Business Administration with a concentration in Organizational Behavior and Strategy Implementation.

Clinton has been intimately involved in working with leadership of all levels of an organization and across all disciplines. This knowledge was a natural transition into executive, business, and career coaching.

Clinton understands organizations and how to interpret the skills and styles of job candidates as well as how they may fit into the company environment. He is committed to supporting your improved performance in your corporate function and your success in planning and achieving your personal career goals by partnering with you in creating and delivering your mission.

THE POWER OF A PERSONAL BRAND

Ellen Zebrun

A personal brand is created with an image, colors, and / or messages used consistently through which you express yourself. A personal brand makes it easier for people to recognize you, identify with you, and choose to engage.

THE IMPORTANCE OF HAVING A PERSONAL BRAND

As a coach, you are in business and more importantly you *are* the business. You are hired because of your ability to ask the powerful and relevant questions that help clients develop priorities, set goals, and establish timelines for those goals. Perhaps you have tangible products such as books or presentations as a component of your coaching business. In any case the core portion of your business is centered on you and what you bring to the table as a coach.

So, what is a personal brand? It is an effective combination of the practical and emotional benefits your services provide, tied together with the unique skills, experience, and personality that are yours alone. Simply put, your personal brand helps you to attract, identify, and serve your target clients more effectively and to streamline the management of your business.

A personal brand serves three critical functions:
1. To empower you being your authentic self
2. To set you apart from your competition
3. To support and increase the growth of your business

Let's take a deeper dive into each of these pieces of the personal brand puzzle.

PERSONAL BRAND AND YOUR AUTHENTIC SELF

With a personal brand, you focus on coaching around your passion, purpose, values, and skills with ease and conviction. When you know yourself and what you offer, you gain recognition for your expertise in your chosen niche. The freeing part of a personal brand is that you get to be you, sharing your values, your personality, and what you as an individual offer your clients.

> *"With a personal brand, you focus on coaching around your passion, purpose, values, and skills with ease and conviction."*

Your personal brand empowers you to communicate clearly about what you do and your process as a coach. This creates clarity for both you and a potential client. For example, there are many career coaches for a person to consider hiring. As a career coach, I focus on mid-career professional women who are stuck in some way; they are either looking to advance their career or make a career transition. Because of how I position myself and communicate who my target client is, people know right away whether I am a good fit for them. They self-identify immediately, "Hey, that's me!" or they recognize that I am not the right coach for them.

When I was a brand new coach, I failed to understand the value of having a personal brand. I was looking for clients everywhere, and was willing to be all things to all people. That approach got me nowhere fast. What are the reasons? Because how I described what I did was so vague, no one was able to connect with what I did as a coach. My wake-up call came one day when a business colleague said, "Ellen, I've known you for a year and I am still not clear on what you do." This was important feedback for me, despite how painful it was to hear. I immediately began to think deeply about my passion, my purpose, and whom I wanted to serve.

A personal brand keeps you focused, just as your mission and vision statements do. You are able to set priorities and goals more easily. Without a solid idea of what is a good fit for you, it's hard to say no to any and all opportunities that come along. With a personal brand you can easily determine whether an opportunity is right. Imagine how many opportunities are offered to Warren Buffet or Oprah on a daily basis. Their unique and individual brand keeps them and those around them, team members, family, and friends, focused on their priorities and goals instead of being distracted by the all of the bright and shiny objects paraded before them.

In a previous life, I was a sales manager; one of the most important concepts I wanted my team to grasp was the importance of getting a yes or no answer from a prospective buyer. We understood what to do if the answer was yes or if the answer was no. Whether yes or no, we were able to move. I emphasized that it was the maybe that leads to spending time and effort without tangible results, spinning their wheels and getting stuck. It is exactly the same concept when applied to opportunities: it may be great, and then your personal brand will help you decide if it's the right one for your business. If yes, jump on it; if no, say no and keep moving in the direction that aligns with you, your goals, and your brand.

YOUR PERSONAL BRAND SETS YOU APART

There are a number of broad areas for you as coach to choose for your business and within each area there are niches. Even within a niche, you still have plenty of competitors wanting to connect with your potential clients. A personal brand sets you

92

apart from your competitors and helps your target clients to easily identify you as the best choice for their purposes.

For example, let's say you are a life coach. A few niches for you to consider are dating, ADHD management, organization, spirituality, time management, and retirement. How can prospective clients tell the difference between you and the others in your niche? Your personal brand clearly articulates what makes you different or more effective than your competitors. This helps your clients identify and connect with you as the right coach for them. When you highlight what makes you unique, you are seen as an individual rather than part of the crowd.

"When you highlight what makes you unique, you are seen as an individual rather than part of the crowd."

With a personal brand, you are more than a commodity where you are selling yourself and your services based on price alone. A personal brand will woo clients based value instead of price. It distinguishes you from your competitors. If a coach is chosen based on price alone people will choose the lower cost every time.

Tied closely to this is client loyalty. With a personal brand people will stay with you because the relationship began based on the unique value you offer. When people are convinced of the value you offer as a coach, they will remain loyal and also be willing to pay higher fees because of the benefit they perceive and receive.

YOUR PERSONAL BRAND SUPPORTS BUSINESS GROWTH

With a personal brand your credibility increases as well. With credibility comes the opportunity to be a thought leader in your niche. The respect and recognition you gain from being a thought leader will attract the kind of clients you desire by showcasing your chosen niche and becoming a specialist. For example, write an article on a specific topic relevant to your niche and then use that article as the foundation for any number of blog posts and podcasts. Then expand that article into a book and create a presentation from your book, and sell the book at your presentations. This will demonstrate your expertise and gain visibility to attract your ideal clients. It will grow your coaching business and position you as a thought leader in your niche.

A successful businessperson knows the importance of gaining new clients primarily through referrals. If a current client can clearly talk about you because of your brand, and how your specialized services made a big difference, then getting referrals will be that much easier. It's very powerful when your current clients endorse you to their friends, family, and co-workers; it means others do your marketing for your business.

This may seem oddly counterintuitive: the more focused you are in your business the lazier you get to be with your marketing. It's easier to create a marketing message when the core is the same. Once you create your message with a logo, color scheme, or graphic format use it every time you send something.

Think of your personal brand as a magnet: the stronger it is, the more powerfully it attracts new clients and retains current ones. Your phone will ring with offers for new opportunities as well because people find you based on your brand. With greater demand for your services, the fees you command increase. This also empowers you to be very intentional about deciding which new clients to take on. It's all about being completely sure of what products to offer, which projects to start, which alliances to pursue, and how to package your offerings.

> *"Think of your personal brand as a magnet:*
> *the stronger it is, the more powerfully it attracts new clients*
> *and retains current ones."*

Personal branding is all about consistency of message, of look, and of format. There is a difference between being consistent and being static. The goal is to balance consistency with keeping things fresh. Using key pieces again and again as your brand and business grow is one way to be consistent; be sure the associated information is kept current and updated. Continue to use these key pieces with your evolving brand as you and your business grow.

Your confidence will soar because of your personal brand. You know your core strengths and abilities, and you know you have something valuable to offer. Focusing on what you want in your business keeps you fulfilled, engaged and moving forward.

> *"Your confidence will soar because of your personal brand."*

A TALE OF TWO COACHES

Let's look at Wilma and Betty, two coaches who each started their coaching business in the past 12 months. They are both career coaches, focusing on people who want to make a transition to a higher-level position.

Wilma has worked hard on her personal brand, which is consistently carried throughout her web site, business card, marketing materials, and tag lines. An avid gardener, Wilma decided to use plants and seeds as her theme. Her colors are shades of green and other vibrant natural colors, her logo is a sprouting plant, and Wilma ensures that her marketing is consistent with this theme.

The taglines that Wilma uses in her marketing messages also refer to gardening and growing things. For example, her blogs and web site will have questions like "Is it time to turn over a new leaf?" or "Do you want to grow in your career?"

Wilma understands that for career advancement, it is vital for clients to have a thorough understanding of their own strengths, values, skills, and desires. She refers to this kind of self-awareness as being rooted or knowing one's roots. Wilma continually emphasizes that career advancement is all about the client planting seeds within his or her network so that future opportunities can bloom.

Early on in her business, Wilma identified her target client: a young professional woman who wants to advance in her field, whether she stays at her current organization or looks for opportunities elsewhere. With this decision, Wilma researched the top challenges for these women and where they looked for resources offering help and support. Wilma then tailored her marketing and networking to those areas.

Visitors to her web site come wanting to stay there and read a blog or sign up for the monthly newsletter because of how

Wilma communicates her identity and services as a coach. Those who visit her website can tell right away that Wilma has something of value to offer. Viewers know immediately whether Wilma is a good fit for them and make decisions accordingly. They like what they see and they interact by filling out the contact request form, signing up for the newsletter, reading, or posting a comment on a blog.

Wilma has been able to raise her fees since starting her business a year ago; this is due to the fact that her clients see her as a valuable resource with the experience and skill to support them as they take control of their career trajectory.

Clients are attracted to Wilma because she communicates clearly who she is, what she does, and how her services help them advance in their careers. Wilma is authentic to her own passions and purpose; she understands that her love of gardening connects deeply with her love of helping people who want to grow and develop.

> *"Clients are attracted to Wilma because she communicates clearly who she is, what she does, and how her services help them advance in their careers."*

Betty is also a career coach who works with people who want to advance their careers.

Once certified as a coach, Betty got her business up and running immediately. She hired a web site designer to create a web site and a graphic designer for her logo and marketing materials. These all look very clean and professional and are also very impersonal. There is nothing that tells a story about Betty; her entire approach is very general in nature. In her desire to attract as many clients as possible, Betty has made the misstep of trying to attract anyone with a pulse. Her taglines and other marketing materials are vague; they are meant to appeal to everyone and the result is that no one connects with them. Potential clients fail to connect themselves or their particular situation to her marketing. Their impression is that Betty is professional, and they have no idea if or how she can support them as individuals.

Betty, in her desire to be seen as professional, has kept her passion and personality out of her marketing materials for her business. Without any kind of personality or target client, a prospective client is unable to connect with Betty on a personal level. Betty failed to recognize that before people will consider hiring her, they want to know, like, and trust her through her marketing. From her materials everyone assumes that she is professional, and therefore potentially trustworthy, and at the same time there is nothing there to help them know or like her on a personal level.

"Without any kind of personality or target client, a prospective client is unable to connect with Betty on a personal level."

Those who land on her web site leave without interacting. Again, because the information is so general and covers so many different topics, there is nothing specific enough for anyone to know if Betty is able to help them in their particular situation.

Betty wants to increase her fees now that she has some experience; her current clients chose her partly because of her low prices. They've referred others to her because she's good, and also because of the lower fees she charges. It's difficult for Betty to justify raising her fees when the conversation revolves around her services being a commodity available to all rather than being designed intentionally for a specific market.

CREATING A PERSONAL BRAND

A personal brand is about establishing your personal vision for you, your family, and your business. Your personal vision is like the mission statement for an organization, it is what separates you from the crowd. This is how you let everyone know who you are, what you do, and how you do it in as personal and authentic a way possible. It is developed through your marketing look and message.

> *"A personal brand is about establishing your personal vision for you, your family, and your business."*

BE AUTHENTIC

As the saying goes, the truth will win. You can work feverishly to present yourself as someone different from whom you really are except you end up fooling no one other than yourself. Your brand must be a true representation of your core values, ethics, skills, and background. If you are unsure about what is true for you, do the hard work of increasing your self-awareness first.

Your genuine enthusiasm for your coaching business offerings and how you help clients define and achieve their goals will shine through when you are authentic. Your energy will be contagious and attract others to you. When people decide to pay you with their hard-earned money, it will be because of who you are instead of because of how great your web site looks.

BE CONSISTENT

Without consistency, you have no credibility. People want to trust that they have chosen the right coach. When you are reliable, your reputation will precede you and be known. This makes it easier for everyone to know, like, and trust you, which is a vital first step to getting hired.

"Without consistency, you have no credibility."

What is the key to consistency? Follow up on everything you say you will do and do it on time. Email the information on a book you mentioned, send your clients their notes within the timeframe you set, call your clients on time, confirm their next session the day before, check in with clients in between sessions when you committed to it, and so forth. This creates an enormous level of trust for your clients in you; people want to feel good about how they are spending their money so being consistent, reliable, and professional goes a long way in doing just that.

BE ALIGNED

Do you know a few folks who thrive on drama and chaos? These people make choices that are a mismatch for their stated purpose and actually keep them from achieving their goals. How they spend their time, the company they keep, and how they conduct themselves creates a disconnection between what they say they want, who they say they are, and how they actually move through the world. To have a solid personal brand, it is imperative that your decisions are intentional: decisions about your time, activities, and the people in your life. Examine closely how you spend your time and on what activities. Do these move you closer to or further away from your goals? Painful as it can be, this may mean cutting ties with people who distract you from your focus. Be sure to make intentional decisions about the people in your life by surrounding yourself with people who support you and lift you up.

SET YOUR VALUES

Being true to your values is essential for authenticity and ultimately happiness. Ever been unhappy in a corporate job? Perhaps it was because the organization claimed to have values around serving the customer and growing the staff, and those values were on paper only; the company's actions did not follow their stated values.

> *"Being true to your values is essential for authenticity and ultimately happiness."*

Values help define what is most important. Consider your values when making decisions like taking on a new client, considering an opportunity, or collaborating with another person. How do you know what are your values? Think about the people, emotions, and situations where you've been the happiest; it is in these spaces where you will find your values. Alternatively, you can research online for assessments around values or authentic happiness. The results will be helpful. The

103

number of values you list is entirely up to you; they are your values, after all.

PRIORITIZE YOUR VALUES

Now that you have your list of values, the next step is to prioritize them. Decisions about your business and your family will be made on a daily basis, so prioritizing values will help. Once you know the values that are most important to you, it will become easier to make decisions. Keeping true to your values will help you find happiness in both your personal and professional lives. It's a balancing act between personal and professional so knowing what makes you happiest will definitely help you.

What is an example of this balancing act? Let's say you are presented with a great opportunity to coach on site for three straight weeks at one of your target companies. This is a good fit for your professional and business growth values. At the same time being on site for three weeks feels too long to be away from your family right now. Because you know your value priorities, you are able to make a decision or even negotiate a situation that works better for you (for example, work on site the first and third weeks then do phone call coaching and/or webinars from home for the second week).

104

IDENTIFY YOUR PASSIONS

Values and passions, aren't they the same thing? No. A value is a core belief. A passion interests you, it makes you want to learn and do more. Passions drive you to get better, both personally and professionally. A passion is what you will do whether a paycheck is involved or not. The best example of someone following her passion is Oprah. Her passion is to help and educate people, which she does on a daily basis through her magazine, the school she established in Africa, and her charity work. Has she made a lot of money in the process? Yes indeed, and that's what happens when you follow your passion.

> *"Passions drive you to get better, both personally and professionally."*

It's important to create two lists for your passions: one is personal and the other is professional. Remember our first coach example, Wilma? She blended her personal passion for gardening into her professional world by use of branding with colors and messages that all connected to gardening. Her marketing materials make her happy whenever she sees them.

Passion is all about what activities you like doing and how you spend your time. Perhaps one of your top values is family; what do you want to do with your family? Does your family like outdoor activities like hiking or camping? Do they prefer to go to the movies or a museum? Maybe part of your family values is date night with your partner once a week.

What are your passions around your business? Maybe you thrive on giving presentations, or you experience fulfillment through writing a blog post or an article. How do you prefer to work? One-on-one or with groups? In person or through on-line resources like webinars? Once you become clear on what fuels your passion, it becomes easier for you to structure your business in order to communicate your passions to potential clients who are like-minded.

> *"…communicate your passions to potential clients …"*

CONCLUSION

As coaches, we are heart-based entrepreneurs who want to impact individuals and organizations in a positive, life-affirming way. A personal brand will clearly show what makes you unique and relevant in a very specific way to your target market. With a clear and consistent message that conveys who you are and how your services and products make a difference in your clients' lives, your powerful personal brand empowers you to reach potential clients easily and effectively. This is how you share your passion and your purpose with others and have the business and future that you want.

Ellen Zebrun is the owner and principal of The Clear Strategy Coach, LLC and focuses on mid-career professional women who want to either advance their current career or transition to a new career. Ellen realizes a personal brand is critical for those in job search or career transition so that they are able to communicate their experience, worth, and interest in a clear, concise, and compelling way. As the Clear Strategy Coach, Ellen partners with her clients as they define their success, identify their goals, and implement their solutions. Passionate about equipping her clients with the confidence and knowledge they want to realize their dream future, Ellen will work side-by-side with you to create a strategy that is unique to your strengths, skills, and values.

Ellen received both her Certified Professional Coach and Certified Master Coach through the Center for Coaching Certification program. She is a member of the International Coach Federation, International Coach Federation Minnesota Chapter, Society of Human Resource Management, and the Association for Talent and Development. Ellen has BA and MFA degrees and is a certified trainer through The Bob Pike Group. Ellen lives in Minneapolis with her husband, their cat and dog, and enjoys when her 26-year-old daughter calls home.

www.TheClearStrategyCoach.com

ACCESSING THE CLIENT NETWORK

Jennifer Mount

As a client embarks on the coaching journey, he or she is often looking to make a change or to grow into the next version of him or herself. This transformation invites the support of others to make the appropriate transitions and to value and accept this new way of being. This validation and acceptance is an important factor to creating tangible results and confirming the new reality. The people who surround the client and hold the new space bring perspective, a comfort level, the connections, and the approval that support the client moving forward. Therefore, it is valuable to ask the client to consider how his or her network will contribute to the process of achieving a goal.

The client's network is a great wealth of knowledge, ideas, encouragement, and stimuli that will build the confidence within the client to take action. The coach can partner with the client to discover how a network can be an inspirational tool for moving forward and accomplishing what they want. The process of accessing the client's network both provides support and resources, and it is also a method for developing effective communication and leadership skills.

There are five steps to accessing the client network: map the network, identify key people, build a trust team, craft trust team requests, and create a plan of action.

> *"There are five steps to accessing the client network: map the network, identify key people, build a trust team, craft trust team requests, and create a plan of action."*

The first step in the process is to ask the client to create a map of every person they know. The map identifies the support systems that the client can utilize as he or she pursues a goal. It also helps to assist the client in recognizing that there are several options in identifying a clear path to success. The second step is to identify the key people who will be the client's greatest asset for mobilizing the client and/or other people around the goal. Step three is to build a trust team of the key people that will provide the resources the client wants to achieve the goal. Step four is to craft trust team requests so the client will be effective and productive in his or her communications with others. The fifth and final step is to create a plan of action for the trust team in assisting the client towards accomplishment and success.

MAP THE NETWORK

A great exercise to utilize during the coaching process is mapping the client's network. Ask the client to categorize the various groups of people they belong to, for example; family, friends, colleagues, classmates, religious groups, etc. Next, the client will add the names of the people he or she knows within each group. This exercise will take time, so I recommend you ask the client if he or she wants to work on the map with you during a session or do it as an assignment. Encourage the client to be creative as he or she draws the map. The client may use colors to signify each group or design a network tree. If you invite the client to be creative, it will make the exercise light and fun. Creativity will also help to distinguish the various groups so the client can easily find a person to connect with when building the trust team. Most importantly, the map will support the client so they feel empowered by discovering their own way of connecting different groups of people together.

There are many resources available online to build a network map such as LinkedIn, Google Circles, and Facebook. These sites may be the easiest and fastest way for some clients to create a network map depending on how often they use social media to connect with others.

The network map has many benefits such as demonstrating to the client that the tremendous support and associations that he or she has are a resource. It also helps the client to identify key players in accomplishing a goal and to clarify who to invite to the trust team.

IDENTIFY KEY PEOPLE

In most cases, the client will ask others to assist in manifesting his or her goals. For example, efforts toward being promoted, taking a leadership role, buying a home, and being healthy are supported with helping hands. The client will name a key person or people within each group that they have designated on the network map for support with their goals. It is important to ask the client to define key people or players for his or herself as this will keep the client in the driver's seat.

If the client struggles to define a key person, you may add perspective for what a key person looks like. Key people are defined as the client's top contributors to moving the client towards success by offering encouragement, completing requested tasks, or connecting the client to other people and/or resources. They may also be defined as those who will be a catalyst for bringing a group of people together, act as a representative of the group as a whole, or take the lead and manage a particular group of people for the client.

> *"Key people are defined as the client's top contributors to moving the client towards success by offering encouragement, completing requested tasks, or connecting the client to other people and/or resources."*

One option is for the coach to invite the client to draw a circle and put a goal in the middle, just like a target. Next, the client will look at their network map and choose people that can offer support around the goal or who will benefit from them accomplishing the goal. It is important for the coach to ask the following questions to guide the client in identifying key players.

- **Who are your Advocates**?

Advocates are people who publicly support or promote something. If the client wants to establish his or herself (for example, as a leader or candidate for a job), advocates are people who will speak on the client's behalf to build credibility.

- **Who are your Super Connectors?**

Super Connectors know a lot of people and/or resources and will connect the client to them.

- **Who are your Leaders?**

Leaders act as the main point of contact for a particular group of people that the client is working to mobilize. The client may ask the leader to motivate and manage this group on the client's behalf.

- **Who are your Delegates?**

Delegates are people that the client may designate to do a specific task.

The client will continue to add layers of rings with more people and/or organizations. Typically, the people who are close to the goal in the center of the circle are those who may be most open to supporting the client. They may also indicate who the client is most comfortable with and who will help to build the client's confidence.

BUILD A TRUST TEAM

After the client has drawn the network map and identified key people to accomplish a goal, the third step is to build a team they trust. This team will empower the client to reach each goal by coordinating the appropriate resources to get there.

For example, the client wants to be seen as a leader at work and chooses this as an individual goal to work towards. The client decides to take action by creating a project that will support accomplishing a company or organizational goal and wants the help of others to promote and work on the project. In short, the client constructs a team. In order to reach a goal, the client will want a team he or she can rely on to do designated tasks and/or support the client's confidence and integrity.

People to consider for the trust team:
- Who inspires you?
- Who motivates you?
- Who makes you feel grounded and calm?

- Who challenges you?
- Who has the listening of others?
- Who is your cheerleader?
- Who has a strength that compliments your weakness?
- Who has the skills?
- Who has access to resources or can make connections?
- Who is or can be your mentor?

The coach will encourage the client to define each person for his or herself. When helpful, the coach adds perspective to stir the client's thinking; here are examples of perspective to offer if the client is stuck to help the client answer these questions.

Who inspires you? A person who inspires causes someone to have a feeling or emotion and often provokes new thinking. This person often offers ideas about what to do or to create.

Who motivates you? A motivator gives the reason to do something and often provides an incentive that motivates action. This person stimulates interest and enthusiasm.

Who makes you feel grounded and calm? Someone who makes another feel calm and grounded is sensible, well balanced, and has a good understanding of what is important in life. He or she assists in getting to a peaceful and quiet emotional state so that the focus is productive and thoughtful.

Who challenges you? (As the client considers who may be a challenger, it is helpful to keep the word challenge positive.) A person who challenges is someone who can offer a different point of view and may play devil's advocate. It is an opportunity to expand awareness and consider another perspective that may be new.

Who has the listening of others? Listening refers to the perceptions of others; a person who has the listening of others can provide perspective on what others believe. Understanding the listening of a group of people will empower taking action in order to transform others perceptions. This person can help shift or change the perceptions appropriately.

Who is your cheerleader? A cheerleader is an enthusiastic and vocal supporter. This person applauds performance and sings the praise about people to others.

Who has a strength that compliments your weakness? This person supports in areas that are less strong and gives balance. For example, if a client's strength is creativity and free thinking, this person will help organize thoughts and provide structure.

Who has the skills? For example, if creating a website for a project, identify a person in the network that is skilled at developing a website.

Who has access to resources or can make connections? This person has a relationship and/or entry point to a person, organization, tools etc. to move closer to a goal.

Who is your mentor? A mentor is an experienced and trusted advisor. He or she can teach, give help, and provide council. This person often has influence because he or she is in a more senior position.

The objective of a trust team is to surround the client with people who will encourage, motivate, inspire, and create a positive environment for the client. A positive environment is essential for the client as he or she attempts to make changes in moving towards a goal. Changes will often take a client out of his or her comfort zone to promote personal growth. The trust team will be there as a support when the going gets tough or goals appear to be impossible. The trust team provides another level of access to what the client wants.

> *"A positive environment is essential for the client as he or she attempts to make changes in moving towards a goal."*

After the client has chosen people for the trust team, it is time to bring the team together. The coach will ask the client to assign a day and time in which he or she will contact each person. It is important for the client to craft a conversation for how he or she will invite people to the trust team.

117

CRAFT TRUST TEAM REQUESTS

Two common barriers to achieving a goal are self-confidence and fear. This is true when building a trust team too because many clients feel awkward in making requests of others, especially if they have selected people that they do not currently have a close relationship with or know well. It may be due to fear of rejection or lack of confidence in the actual request. The coach will surface obstacles in the way of the client when asking others to be on the trust team. These obstacles are often consistent with other road blocks that prevent the client from moving forward, so it is beneficial to work through them. For example, if the client struggles with self-confidence, the coach may recommend a separate coaching session dedicated to building confidence. In this session, the coach and the client will walk through areas in which the client feels confident and uncover the areas in which they have experienced success. The client will gain self-assurance as he or she recognizes all that has been accomplished and the tools used to get there. The client can then apply these tools to the situations in which they do not feel confident and/or develop new tools with the coach. A session or conversation dedicated to moving past a barrier or building a skill will ensure the client is on the path to success.

> *"A session or conversation dedicated to moving past a barrier or building a skill will ensure the client is on the path to success."*

Once the client has worked through challenges in making requests of others, it is time to set a date and time to connect with each member of the trust team. Coach the client on how to approach each person. Consider asking the following questions:

- What qualities or aspects inspired you to ask this person?
- How will you connect with this person?
  - What is the foundation of the relationship?
  - How will you build rapport before making the request?
- How will this person be an asset to you?
- How will you be an asset to them?
- What role will this person play on the trust team?
- What is the opportunity in supporting you?
- How will you attract this person to your trust team?
- What will you say when you make the request to join the trust team?

If the client does not currently have a relationship with the person he or she is inviting, the coach will assist in uncovering how the client can gain access to this person and then establish a foundation for the request. For example:

- Who will make an introduction to this person for you?
- Who has influence with this person?
- How will you introduce yourself?

- What will you say to provide the person with your background, experience, and foundation for the invitation?
- What do you want moving forward?

If the coach surfaces this thinking beforehand, the client will build confidence, gain clarity, and open a space for invitations to the trust team to occur and be successful. The coach may also encourage the client to do a mock conversation. This conversation provides practice and empowers the client to be in the moment of the conversation to see how it feels, looks, sounds, etc. The coach will support the client in improving the invitation as the client sees fit.

The coach will listen for things that may be missing when the client is making the request and then follow up with the above questions again, as appropriate. For example, has the client created a connection with the person? If the client comes running out of the gate with a request instead of building a foundation of rapport, the person may feel apprehensive or not see the value he or she brings to the table. The coach will ask the client, "How will you develop the connection with this person before making the request?" The coach will also look to see if the client has been specific enough in the request so as to provide clarity about what the client is asking. Therefore, the coach will surface the question of what role this person will

120

play and what the opportunity is for him or her. The coach will pay attention to how the request lands and offer questions that will assist the client in continuing to craft an effective invitation. The point is for the client to create an influential and motivating request that is clear and concise.

> *"The point is for the client to create an influential and motivating request that is clear and concise."*

CREATE AN ACTION PLAN

The following questions will serve to create a plan of action for each person on the trust team and the trust team overall. The questions are also tools for effective communication and demonstrating leadership.

- How will being a part of the trust team benefit them?
- What are the goals for the trust team?
  - What are the goals for each person on the team?
- What are the expectations for each person?
- What is the timeline to achieve these goals?
- How often and when will you meet with each person or as a group?
- How will you communicate?
  - For example, what is the client's and the person's preferred method of communication? Email, in person meeting, phone conversation, text, etc.

- What are the specific actions that each person will take and when will he or she take them?
- What may stand in the way of achieving the goal and how will the team move past it?
- How will you measure the success of each relationship and the team?
- How will you celebrate accomplishing the goal?

These questions are very common examples in the coaching process and also serve to aid the client in powerful and effective conversations plus stepping into a role of leadership. Good communication is a key to inviting people to the trust team and, as you can imagine, is a vital tool throughout all of life. The questions empower the client to be thoughtful and strategic about what he or she will say and do so they move forward with confidence.

The action plan will serve as a progress report for the client and the trust team. It will identify barriers to success and methods to moving past these obstacles. As you can see, the coach can branch the conversation on accessing the network into the traditional coaching process of moving a client towards achieving a goal.

> *"The action plan will serve as a progress report for the client and the trust team."*

CONCLUSION

The process of accessing the client's network is a beneficial exercise for the coach to utilize with a client to reveal potential support and resources to accomplishing a goal. The coach can flex and adapt the network process to the level of engagement that the client wants from his or her people. For example, the client may have an individual goal of losing 30 pounds and put a small team of people in place to provide accountability, encouragement, and the knowledge to achieve the goal. This process can also be taken to an organizational level in which a leader or manager is building a team of employees to reach a company goal.

This process develops valuable communication skills, builds strong relationships, and creates an opportunity for the client to be a leader. This process and the skills obtained within the progression provide practice, confidence, and courage on the road to success. Over time, the client will recognize the process as a simple and effective way to accomplish what he or she wants. The client will feel empowered and inspired to take on what he or she desires.

Accessing the client network is also a tremendous opportunity for the coach to consider. The process both provides a way for the coach to have an engaging and successful relationship with the client and also may surface potential coaching prospects. As the client invites his or her network into the trust team and puts each person into action, these people will get an introduction to the coaching process. It is a way to expand your coaching services and obtain referrals from a trustworthy and credible source.

It is a natural evolution for the people in the client's life to observe the progress the client is making and to be curious about the driving force behind the client's transformation and success. The client will engage in numerous conversations on the coach's behalf simply by inviting people to be a part of his or her coaching experience. The coach may choose to invite the client to surface with each person what opportunity this person sees for him or herself in the trust team and/or the coaching process. The coach can offer a free introductory coaching session to the people that express interest in the coaching process. The coach can also offer a free coaching session or some other incentive to the client to generate referrals. Word of mouth is an excellent marketing and advertising tool that stands in complete integrity and calls for minimal additional effort on the part of the coach.

> *"It is a natural evolution for the people in the client's life to observe the progress the client is making and to be curious about the driving force behind the client's transformation and success."*

Another way to increase value for the client and build your business is to offer group coaching sessions to the client and the trust team. The trust team will see firsthand how the coach operates and how the coaching process works. It will also manage the number of free introductory coaching sessions that the coach will dedicate time to offering. A group coaching session will create awareness of other coaching opportunities that exist amongst the group. Be aware of using this opportunity appropriately as one of your coaching services.

The exercise of tapping into the client's network is a win-win-win scenario. The client wins the support and the resources to achieve a goal. The trust team wins both the growth experience through participation and the knowledge and the awareness of how the coaching process may benefit them. The coach wins by providing the client with a successful relationship and also opportunities to increase business. It creates a collaborative effort in achieving personal and collective goals.

ACCESSING THE CLIENT NETWORK PROCESS SUMMARY

- Map the client's network by categorizing groups of people and the individual names of people in each group.
- Identify key players in each group and the people who can support achieving a goal.

- Build a trust team of people who will provide a positive environment and resources.
- Choose a date and time to invite each person to the trust team.
- Craft requests to the people who will be invited.
- Practice a mock conversation to a person on the trust team.
- Create an action plan for the trust team and each individual member.
- Discover opportunities for people in the trust team to be transformed by being on the trust team and through the coaching process.
- Generate business through individual or group coaching sessions for the trust team.

Variety is the spice of Jennifer Mount's life. She holds a Bachelor of Arts in Secondary Education and Spanish from Providence College as well as a MBA from the University of San Francisco. Jennifer is a Certified Master Coach through the Center for Coaching Certification and a member of the International Coaching Federation. She has experience with healthcare marketing, hospitality, financial, and advisory services and has partnered with startups, non-profits, and global corporations. Her expertise spans call center, client and talent management, marketing, sales, and learning and development. As the Associate Director of Global Learning Design at CEB, Jennifer designed leadership development programs for Fortune 500 companies. During her time as a Client Manager with Fidelity Investments, Jennifer managed the strategic and operational objectives of clients.

Jennifer married her experiences and followed her passion as the founder of OptU Possibility where she creates the time, space, and support for people to reflect, discover, and map their individual leadership path. Jennifer is also co-founder of The Collaborative SF which creates programs to develop women leaders with the integration of mind, body, and spirit. She enjoys dancing, hiking, surfing, cooking, connecting, and travel.

Jennifer@OptUPossibility.com

COACHING MILLENNIALS

Tim Dean

Millennials. Just the word conjures up a wide range of stereotypes, as well as both negative and positive perceptions. From narcissistic praise junkies who expect immediate rewards to multi-tasking entrepreneurs who want to make a real difference in the world, Millennials have been the topic of dozens of articles and books for some time now. It makes sense. As of 2015, Millennials represent the largest generation in terms of population size and number in the workforce.

From the G.I. Generation (born 1901-1924) and Traditionalists (1925-1945) to Baby Boomers (1946-1964) and Generation X (1965-1980), every generation has a name. So what defines a generation? Age? Experiences? Core Values? Something else? While several informational resources define a generation by birth years, for purposes of this chapter, I prefer to expound on that definition to include events that shaped a generation's psyche. Like many authors and experts, I am defining a generation as: a birth cohort; a group of people who share a common characteristic or experience across social, political, economic, and technological events.

When it comes to Millennials (also known as Generation Y, born 1981-1999) we have heard the labels combined frequently with doom-and-gloom consequences: Millennials are entitled, lazy, distracted, and unrealistic; Millennials are the "me" generation; Millennials cannot interact face to face; Millennials will be the downfall of society. Is there a different possibility?

First, this mindset sounds very familiar. Growing up in the 1970s and 1980s, I remember hearing over and over again how my generation, the slackers of Generation X, would "bring about the end of business and civilization as we know it."

In a leadership workshop I developed and deliver each year to post-graduate students, I recommend that rather than falling prey to these negative Millennial stereotypes, as well as equally prevalent negative stereotypes for the other generations, they instead connect via individual strengths, unique working styles, and interaction preferences that exist for *all* generations. In fact, there is more common ground across the generations than many realize. For example, a multi-decade research survey confirmed that each generation desires the same intrinsic values: meaningful work, learning opportunities, and being challenged. Plus, it is very common to hear older generations say that a younger generation is narcissistic. The reality? Every generation is a "me" generation. Every generation of younger people is perceived as more narcissistic than their elders. It is simply a given. The bottom line? Understanding more about each generation can provide clues to establishing better connections and achieving more productive interactions. Yes, with Millennials too.

> *"...connect via individual strengths, unique working styles, and interaction preferences that exist for all generations."*

WHO ARE THESE MILLENNIALS?

Millennials are recognized as one of the most civic-minded generations who, unlike older generations, also possess a strong sense of community on a global scale. Whether at work or at play, they want to be a part of something bigger than themselves. Plus their definition of a job has taken on a whole new meaning.

Four generations are working together now and this is a new phenomenon. By 2020, a 5th generation, Generation Z, will be added to the mix. True, many older workers are delaying retirement, some by choice to stay active and alert, while others, for financial necessity, have to remain on the job. Even still, Baby Boomers continue to retire at a pace of 10,000 workers every day. Typically, as the older generation retires, the next generation steps up to fill all of the employment gaps. There is a problem: the generation after Baby Boomers, Generation X, does not have enough workers to fill all of the vacant employee and leadership spots. Not by a long shot.

Today, there are approximately 66 million Americans considered to be Generation X, while Baby Boomers – the largest generation in our history until 2014 – total more than 70 million.   Even if every working Generation X employee replaced every retiring Baby Boomer employee in the workforce, the gap will still be significant.   Therefore, Millennials, with more than 77 million to their ranks, and growing each year, will lead sooner and younger than any generation before them.

Combined with the fact that Millennials are the most globally aware generation, they possess a desire to make the world a better place.   As such, Millennials are poised to make a true impact on the corporate landscape, and consequently, are uniquely positioned to change the way we think about the business world.

As the first global generation, Millennials witnessed world events in real time.   Thanks to technology and the internet, Millennials have been exposed to dozens of global events – good and bad – as they are happening.   From a country's first democratic election to civil rights violations in China, Millennials are there with their brethren, being a part of the experience together as it unfolds.   Closer to home, for many Millennials, 9/11 ignited their desire to make a difference.   On that fateful day, Millennials saw their world come down, literally and figuratively. They now want to build it back up. They want to connect. In fact, they crave making connections.

True, many of us as kids probably felt the same way and had similar thoughts. "When I grow up, I want to make a difference," we said. To be fair, a lot of young people tend to be more idealistic. How many of us actually acted on it? For many Millennials, they feel almost obligated to have a positive impact on their community, their country, and yes, even their world. Because they process information differently than older generations, they are adaptable thinkers and possess a jack-of-all-trades learning mindset. It is this combined heroic spirit and interest for continuous learning about the world, and themselves, that have made Millennials an incredibly receptive generation to coaching.

> *"It is this combined heroic spirit and interest for continuous learning about the world, and themselves, that have made Millennials an incredibly receptive generation to coaching."*

WHAT MAKES MILLENNIALS SO COACHABLE?

For years, generations actually, parents have been raising kids with a very common, over-arching edict: do well in school, earn good grades to get accepted into college, leverage an undergraduate degree to land a well-paying job, get promoted, manage a team, then a division, and, if you are lucky enough, manage an entire company. It was basically all planned out. Ultimately, if you work your way up the corporate ladder, you will successfully reach the pinnacle of earning six figures (at least) with your fellow deserving executives who advanced via the same expected career path.

I can certainly relate to this journey. Like my college-educated older four siblings, I was taught to study hard in high school to get accepted to the college of my choice. Doing so, I graduated with a degree in engineering because I knew an engineering degree would pay well. Even when I changed major my junior year, I was adamant about remaining in the college of engineering to sustain the projected payout. Upon graduation, as planned, I landed a high-paying position for a global corporation. As so on and so on.

To some, this parenting philosophy of bringing up children where success is defined by the same pre-defined accomplishments is ideal. To others the perpetual repetition of simply raising kids the same way as the previous generation is limiting. When does it ever change? Where ever your allegiances lie, Millennials are all about exploring what they truly desire and continue doing so throughout their career path.

"Millennials are all about exploring what they truly desire and continue doing so throughout their career path."

This younger exploration, and pursing it, is, in part, a result of the 24/7 (24 hours a day, 7 days a week) access to information. Think about it. For Baby Boomers and Generation X, news was delivered twice a day: once in the morning via a newspaper and once in the evening via one of three national 30-mintue news programs. Because of technology, Millennials have been consuming news, global news, all day, every day, throughout their entire lives.

A second factor that has created a coachable generation is the dramatic shift in the coaching practice itself. In the recent past, if your boss approached you and mentioned coaching, it might have been met with resistance. Perhaps getting a coach meant something was wrong or a perceived negative behavior needed to be addressed. In fact, having a coach in the 1970s and 1980s meant a final attempt to save your job and also proliferated a negative stigma of being labeled as broken, and judged by professional peers in a way that was associated with psychotherapy. Conversely, Millennials welcome coaching as simply an extension of their upbringing and continued growth. This mindset has helped facilitate a 180-degree change in how coaching is perceived by society. Instead of a reactionary "fix this or your gone" implementation, coaching, for both personal and professional advancement, is now recognized as a proactive, career building and life-affirming ingredient for continued growth and ongoing success.

Finally, to further understand the reasons Millennials are open and receptive to coaching, go back several decades to when their parents were children and young adults themselves. Throughout the 1960s and early 1970s, the family dynamic consisted of a one-working parent household with Dad at work and Mom at home. Then in the late 1970s, that dynamic started shifting to a dual-working environment with both parents earning a paycheck. In addition, divorce rates were on the rise, which created a home environment where neither parent was available until early evening. In essence, Generation X constantly shuttled from one parent to another (hence the "latchkey generation" label) and recognized the only person they could count on was themselves. As such, they decided early on that when they became parents and had children of their own, now known as the Millennial generation, both parents being visible, available, and accessible 24/7 is a priority.

Continuous advancements in technology such as virtual offices, telecommuting, and video conferencing, combined with a proactive spike for more work-life-balance across corporate America, further provided the perfect scenario for both Mom and Dad to raise, and mentor, their Millennial kids from birth. One result is a concept called helicopter parenting, where both parents hovered over their kids like a helicopter, raising a generation of, wait for it, dependent narcissists. More realistic is to discover that this present-day assist from Mom and Dad actually began many years ago and is merely a continuation of a parenting style that was initiated decades earlier. Bottom line: Millennials like to be coached and, in fact, have been coached one way or the other their entire lives.

> *"Millennials like to be coached and, in fact, have been coached one way or the other their entire lives."*

WHAT'S IN IT FOR MOM AND DAD?

Time and again, every parent I coach expresses the same goal: a happy and healthy child. For parents of Millennials, a new wrinkle has emerged that many of these parents did not expect or anticipate: having their adult child move back home. Remember, these parents want to continue being a supportive role model for their child. At the same time, the parents assumed their children would follow in the same education and career path they did: high school, college, new job, move out, etc. Instead their children, now young adults, are contemplating what to do with their new diploma and have moved back home to do it.

An unprecedented result is the rise in young adults living in a multi-generational household. In fact, close to 30 percent of all Millennials in the U.S. now live with their parents, a percent of returning nesters not seen since the 1940s. Comparatively,

Baby Boomers returned home at a rate of 5 percent while Gen Xers moved back at a rate of 11 percent. (In Canada, it is estimated roughly one-half of Millennials still live with their parents.)

So with nearly a third of Millennials now living back home, the parents are experiencing a combination of equal parts loving determination with, at times, exhaustive exacerbation that comes from raising, and for many, now living with their Millennial children again. Underneath that frustration, however, lies the supportive, helicopter-hovering parent Millennials feel most comfortable around. Whether by necessity or choice, Millennials have found themselves back in the supportive and collaborative environment they grew up with: Mom and Dad willing to help and wanting to coach. Deciding to hire a coach like myself for their Millennial son or daughter merely continues their parenting mantra. For many it also jump starts the process of getting their home back to themselves.

WHAT IS IT LIKE TO COACH MILLENNIALS?

Millennials, especially in this new millennium, are very much aware of globalization. With more and more Millennials migrating to the United States every year (the reason their ranks in the United States continue to rise) it is important to consider that international Millennials were raised in different parenting circumstances. As such, it is completely understandable that immigrant Millennials – age-identical to their U.S. counterparts – possess differing views, values, and influences based primarily on their geography. For the purposes of this section, I focus specifically on Millennials raised in the United States.

Unlike older generations, Millennials grew up during the dawn of the internet. As a result, they had (and continue to have) access to hundreds of online social platforms, 24/7, to share their lives. While some will debate their look-at-me rationale and perceived happiness persona, many Millennials have developed an inward self-awareness which is completely different. This internally-focused self-consciousness has surfaced with every Millennial client I have coached.

It makes sense when you think about. How often have you been to a sporting event or music concert where all you see are fans recording and posting the scene taking place right in front of them? In lieu of being in the moment and enjoying the event as it unfolds, audience members are taking time to click, crop, and like selfie photos that each one of them and their friends, who are literally right next to them, just posted. They are posting about something they actually did not truly experience. It has reached a point where recording artist Adam Levine recently requested that his concert fans at a Ft.

Lauderdale, Florida venue turn off their phones. He asked his audience to experience a moment as a group without technology.

As my Millennial clients have shared, they want to establish and convey a more honest and individual identity. As opposed to letting others determine their self-worth based on the number of followers, retweets, or likes, they want to take back their own happiness. They also seek out self-development opportunities and want to discuss goals that are, at times, out of sync with conventional wisdom and the aforementioned career/life path they were encouraged to follow. Combine this with their unwavering desire to better our world and have a significant role in it and you can further understand how Millennials are uniquely poised to bring about monumental change and for some, to become tomorrow's great leaders.

> *"...they want to establish and convey a more honest and individual identity."*

In addition, while Millennials are now the most educated generation ever, they were raised by the most educated parents at that time. Who better to ask advice about college, career, and life choices then the older generation who experienced a similar journey? (Conversely, my grandfather quit school for good after the seventh grade and became a fireman to support his family. While a wonderful role model and second father, he lacked applicable experiences to warrant a helpful or relevant perspective.)

Regarding my Millennial clients: I have discovered common top-priority goals surface depending on the Millennial's age. The youngest Millennials, ages 19-24, tend to focus their highest priority on finding their first (or next) job. Millennials who are 25-29 identify more financial-related goals first, like saving to buy a home or to schedule that dream vacation. Finally, starting a family and settling down are the top goals for Millennials 30-34. Holistically, this goals-by-age pattern is understandable and is what I refer to as the three Fs in a Millennial's young adult journey: Field, Finances, and Family. For the vast majority of Millennials that I coach, further evidence to an earlier point, it has been their parents who initiated the coaching engagement.

MILLENNIALS: THREE FS

The following are based on true stories; the client names, revealing details, and minor facts have been changed to protect confidentiality.

At 23, Zack had already left two professional positions in a span of eight months. His Dad, concerned that Zack's performance and behavior were possible contributing factors, called me to discuss how coaching could help with Zack's latest job search. While other goals were relevant, Zack's number one priority was finding the next job in his area of expertise, his field. Zack's personality was reserved while his intent of working with me was laser focused. I was impressed with his level of maturity and his ability to take time to think before he talked. (What percent of 23 year olds do that?) A reserved thinker, Zack took a moment to reflect on each question before giving his answer. Like many Millennials I had met, Zack's openness to coaching was evident from day one. He welcomed the support and was receptive to the process.

Cory had recently graduated college at the age of 27. Like Zach, Cory's father contacted me to help his son be more intentional and accountable regarding his job search. Also like Zack, Cory's goals included securing his next position. Cory's top priorities focused on saving for his own apartment, paying down debt, and putting aside a small fund for a well-deserved vacation. For Cory, it started with his Finances. Even though he and Zach were both looking for employment, Cory was adamant about making sure that while his job mattered, his financial house mattered more. Cory possessed a unique tandem of thinking strategically and communicating persuasively which proved paramount for crafting his resume and producing his portfolio.

I had been friends with Matt for years before he contacted me about coaching. Matt's interest, at age 31, focused on his wife and their first child due in seven months. For him, his career was great and his finances stable, even with the required budgeting adjustments called for with a new baby along the way. Matt's number one goal and focus were his new daughter and his Family. Matt was realizing the new baby was going to change his life forever, literally. He also felt it time to, as he put it, act more like an adult. (It is interesting to note his thinking gels with a recent national survey of Millennials who were asked at what age they believe people become an adult. The top answer was age 30.) While Matt's father did not initiate contact (Matt did), his father played, and continues to play, a critical support role in Matt's ongoing progress.

These age-specific similarities facilitate awareness and effective feedback for existing Millennial clients, and indirectly, for their parents. Understandably, common goals afford relevant insights for ongoing and future coaching clients. The general interests are relevant knowledge and perspective to share, in generalities of course, with Mom and Dad. This information reinforces the parents' decision to hire a coach in the first place.

"Understandably, common goals afford relevant insights for ongoing and future coaching clients."

WHAT DOES THE FUTURE HOLD?

The Millennial generation cares. They care about their society. They care about their connectedness. They care about what each other thinks. In fact, close to three-fourths of Millennials feel more excited about a decision they have made when their friends agree with them.

If you ask a Millennial what they want to do, you will understandably get a variety of answers. If you dig deeper and ask the reasons they want do it, you will begin to hear a shared and common response: to make a positive impact on the world. This generation is very passionate about getting involved, both on and off the job. In lieu of the status associated with working for a Fortune 500 company, Millennials place more value on what a company is doing to make the world a better place or how that company is giving back to society. Millennials want to work for a company with a cause, a company that practices philanthropic outreach and encourages volunteerism. As you can imagine, coaching Millennials through this professional exploration and personal validation is extremely rewarding.

Millennials. Yes, even the word conjures up a range of perceptions and emotions. Remember that Millennials want the same things in life as you and I. They simply communicate it differently.

144

While not a parent myself, I hear many parents say that all they truly want is for their children to be happy and healthy. Millennial's happiness, in a large part, comes from making a difference and having a positive impact on their world and society. Plus, because of technology, we are now in a unique skill set paradigm. For the first time, older generations (Gen X and Boomers) are turning to a younger generation (Millennials) to learn things. Where for decades we looked to our elders, apprentices, older teachers, parents, etc., for learning, we now rely on Millennials to teach and show us the way.

So if you find yourself frustrated managing a Millennial, or simply having a conversation with one, connect with the individual instead of the stereotype. Begin to consciously shift your thinking from self-absorbed narcissist to self-aware change agent. They have been thinking that way since birth, and their lifelong openness and receptivity to coaching is a big outcome from it. With more than 77 million Millennials, and increasing in number every year, imagine what our world will be like when they are encouraged to pursue a truer purpose. Imagine the potential. As a professional Millennial coach, I do. Every single day.

> *"With more than 77 million Millennials, and increasing in number every year, imagine what our world will be like when they are encouraged to pursue a truer purpose. Imagine the potential."*

Tim Dean, CPC is an international coach and recognized expert for empowering Millennials to maximize their professional and personal potential. A certified facilitator, motivational speaker, and author, Tim has inspired hundreds of Millennials to create the life they want to live. With extensive leadership and executive expertise in talent management, manufacturing, agriculture, energy, and healthcare, Tim brings a unique balance and powerful mix of strategy, creativity, and real-world business insight to every coaching engagement.

Tim holds a Master of Science degree in Industrial Administration from the Tepper School of Business at Carnegie Mellon University (CMU) and a Bachelor of Science degree in Industrial Engineering from the Pennsylvania State University. Tim created and delivers Generational Diversity, as a key component of Tepper's Accelerate Leadership Program to compliment CMU's MBA curriculum. Tim is an adjunct professor for the John Cook School of Business at St. Louis University. His course, Leveraging Generational Differences, teaches Millennial graduate students how to address the real challenges they face as younger managers motivating older employees as well as how to create a working environment that promotes the success of each team member regardless of age.

www.TheCoachingDean.com

Coaching for Dating Success
Michael Zaytsev

Human relationships require effective communication. Even a brief interaction such as ordering a cup of coffee requires a complex series of verbal, physical, and emotional communication that result in a meaningful, if temporary, relationship. Without effective communication, you and the barista are simply two people staring at each other, each wondering what the other wants.

Communication and Confidence: The Foundation

Communication is especially essential to romantic relationships. Successful relationships require a high quality of effective communication. Even the brief relationship with a barista at the coffee shop revolves largely around whether he or she can satisfy your demand for coffee and you can satisfy their requirement that you pay for it. Dating requires many more levels of complexity in communication. Sensing attraction, building trust, asking for a date, initiating intimacy, and other parts of the dating process rely on various communication skills.

For your client to achieve their personal definition of dating success, whatever that may be, calls for communicating effectively and authentically both with their partner or date and also with themselves. Moving past fears with confidence impacts their communication and the process. Support them knowing what they want and what they bring to the table. This is because in many parts of the dating process they will express their desires and values to their partner.

Generally we think of relationships as units of at least two people. Before someone masters the art of relationships with others, first ensure a successful relationship with self. Coaching is a great instrument in developing that relationship. The reflective and introspective nature of the coaching process will help the client define their values, priorities, and goals. Having this clarity of purpose empowers them to better choose the kind of relationships to pursue with others and how they want those relationships to function. This understanding of who they are and what they want will fuel authentic action.

When asked what qualities people find attractive in potential mates, confidence is one of the most popular answers. Confidence is sexy. What is behind this perception? While there is more than one correct answer to that question, this chapter will make the case that the answer has to do primarily with communication. In fact, confidence itself (or a lack of it) is a powerful form of communication because it comes across in your verbal and nonverbal communication.

149

Confidence is the embodiment of authenticity, which is an integral part of effective communication. Even if he or she does not know what the right thing is, a confident person is able to do something that gets them closer to the right thing. For example, if you're back at the coffee shop and you are unsure of what you want, confidence is striding up to the barista and saying, "Hi. I really want a drink and I have no idea which one I want."

This ability to say exactly what you want respectfully, even if what you want is finding out what you want, opens a chapter of sincere communication. Simply explaining a unique, concrete purpose facilitates and invites effective communication, laying the groundwork for a relationship. This is essential for a successful romance.

> *"Confidence is the embodiment of authenticity, which is an integral part of effective communication."*

DEVELOP COMMUNICATION SKILLS

Any significant human endeavor, from running a marathon to composing a beautiful symphony, is the result of learning and action. Even a person who is born with natural talents, a favorable physique, or an ear for music, is well served to develop these gifts on a daily basis.

The same way athletes work out and train their muscles, humans can systematically train and improve their communication skills. Regardless of the current level of communication abilities, each person will benefit by consistently honing and expanding the scope of skills.

Please note: we all have been applying communication skills on a daily basis. This means you have years of communication experience! If you were able to perform the complicated set of actions to acquire this book, you are already a capable communicator ready to apply these skills in a coaching relationship for dating success. Remember, for practice to be helpful it makes sense that it involves practicing the right way. If someone has been communicating poorly for years, the communication process will be less effective than what is possible. Working with a coach helps uncover and correct blind spots.

It is important to identify communication strengths, areas for improvement, habits to redefine, and tendencies under stress. In stressful situations communication styles often change from how they are otherwise. Successful relationships are the ones that can survive and even thrive through times of stress. Thus an understanding of your communication style in times of stress, and the ability to share this information with a potential partner, goes a long way in maintaining partnership. For example, some

151

people become more direct when under pressure, while others become reserved in times of anxiety. Think about how communication changes when stressed. Pay attention and learn from the patterns.

This awareness will help your clients be more in tune with a partner's communication style. Understanding how to treat someone or show compassion in the times when he or she is stressed builds compassion and closeness.

> *"Understanding how to treat someone or show compassion in the times when he or she is stressed builds compassion and closeness."*

GROWTH OCCURS OUTSIDE THE COMFORT ZONE

Just as the athlete pushes and strains his muscles in order for them to grow, a person going beyond what is comfortable will attain meaningful growth. For coaches, it may be helpful to find out where your clients feel comfortable in dating and where they feel uncomfortable. Together, explore the sources of discomfort and ways to overpower it. During a coaching session identify exercises the client can perform to build strong communication muscles. Like with weight training, it's important to start with a manageable load, one that will stretch the client's communication muscle, and get several repetitions.

Begin with easy wins and build momentum. For example, if a client is having trouble approaching potential partners, a good exercise might be saying hello to five strangers every day. What might feel like a huge burden day one will seem easier by day seven. The progress will encourage further exertion in future exercises. These experiences on the edge of and outside the comfort zone are the ones that build ability and confidence.

> *"These experiences on the edge of and outside the comfort zone are the ones that build ability and confidence."*

CONFIDENCE RESULTS FROM EXPERIENCE

A person may have all of the appropriate communication skills to begin a dating relationship, and lack the confidence to do so. What is confidence? Confidence is having certainty about an outcome or capability. Sometimes this confidence is false, such as when someone believes they will win the lottery. Confidence in dating is the belief that for a certain action there will be a corresponding result. If the confidence or lack thereof is false, coaching is a way to support taking appropriate risks. In the lottery, we take a small financial risk for a potential payout of millions; in dating, we take an emotional risk for an emotional reward. Fortunately, your chances of success in dating are exponentially higher than your odds in the lottery!

FROM COMMUNICATION AND CONFIDENCE TO VULNERABILITY

Vulnerability is another way to describe emotional risk. Engaging in a meaningful interaction with another person involves vulnerability.

It seems like the ultimate paradox: the essence of confidence is vulnerability. Communicating a truth about one's self is opening up to another person and giving them permission to express their truth as well. Prepare clients to open up to someone else by first supporting them to open up to them self. Invite them to be honest and open about what motivates them, what they desire, and what they want. By acknowledging these desires and their worthiness to have them, you empower them to take the courageous action to attain them.

Although people subconsciously know truths about themselves, identifying and affirming them is an important part of the confidence building process. There is a moment where one of the two individuals in a potential romantic situation makes his or her intentions known. This communication is instrumental as in some ways it defines what form the future relationship will take. To under-communicate your intention or desires is to create room for uncertainty. Without confidence in the relationship and its potential, both people are less likely to put their best efforts forward in building the relationship.

154

Life is sometimes a gamble. Even a relatively certain situation has a degree of inherent uncertainty. We brave the risks of driving or even walking outside in order to achieve certain life goals and desires. Likewise, it is important to take emotional risks in order to achieve meaningful emotional goals. Although it is challenging to know how another person might react to a romantic proposition, failing to ask will certainly bring no response at all. Vulnerability requires confidence and effective communication and it also breeds trust.

> *"…it is important to take emotional risks in order to achieve meaningful emotional goals."*

COACHING FOR DATING SUCCESS

The coaching process is effective in improving dating results because it simultaneously develops communication skills, builds confidence, supports vulnerability, and helps a client better understand his or her own version of dating success. Amongst other things the coach:

- Creates a space for the client to explore and better understand his or her dating life.
- Helps the client identify which skills and experiences will lead to better results.

- Challenges the client to take action outside of their comfort zone.
- Asks the client to identify and eliminate limiting beliefs.
- Measures progress along the way.
- Reminds the client of his or her desired results.
- Celebrates success with the client.

WHAT DO YOU WANT FROM DATING?

This is the question that begins the dating coaching conversation. A client that is committed to real progress and the coaching process will come into this conversation with some dissatisfaction about their current state of being, or perhaps with concern about the future. It is critically important to understand where the client is, where they want to be, and what future they envision in dating or romance. Concurrently this discussion will be helping to build the client's confidence.

> *"It is critically important to understand where the client is, where they want to be, and what future they envision in dating or romance."*

For example: What are the client's thoughts about settling down or marrying? What is the intention around dating? For example: causal socializing, to get over an old flame, or to meet interesting people. What is causing dissatisfaction today?

156

What stands in the way of dating success? What is working well? How will dating success impact other areas of life? How important is it to achieve dating success? What will that success look and feel like? Whatever the answers, dig deeper. What is driving this desire? What is motivating this goal? Get to the essence of what the client is looking for in their dating.

These are examples of the questions to explore early on in the coaching conversation. The answers will help the client and coach co-create the coaching process and support the client developing their plan of action. They will also help the coach determine the client's level of communication skills.

EXPLORE CLIENT CONFIDENCE

What beliefs does your client have about dating? Identify the limiting ones and ask for permission to challenge them and dig into them. Explore varied perspectives. Ask clients about the numerous positive outcomes that are possible. Identify emotional risks and vulnerabilities to explore where the client is especially sensitive.

Explore what outcomes will give them feelings of great confidence and joy. The answers to this question, especially

157

the adjectives used, will provide important insight about what the client wants.

Also, look for cues of where your client has room for improved confidence. Specific aspects of dating can be scary or frustrating to people. Common examples are fear of rejection, not knowing what to say, not knowing how to start a romantic relationship, or not knowing how to choose who to date. The key is to bring awareness to the client. Once clients are able to see and understand their fears, they are able to begin taking action towards overcoming them. Consider activities or exercises to develop greater confidence.

Of course, confidence develops over time. If you were asked to do something you've never done before, how confident would you be in your ability to do so successfully? What if you were asked to do something you've done thousands of times? For example, how confident would you be about rewiring a toaster as opposed to brushing your teeth? Inspire your clients to enjoy the learning process as a stepping-stone to the dating success they desire.

"Inspire your clients to enjoy the learning process as a stepping-stone to the dating success they desire."

WHAT MUSCLES ARE TO BE EXERCISED FOR DATING?

The communication muscles are the number one group responsible for dating success. This work takes on many forms. First, the client starts by communicating effectively with themselves. They have an understanding of their goals, values, what qualities are appropriate in a partner, what kind of relationship is desired, how much commitment they want to make, and many other decisions. The self-awareness muscles are sure to be exercised regularly in the coaching process. Checking in with a coach, answering questions, and reflecting on actions taken will accomplish this and build the communication muscle along with awareness. Journaling is another powerful tool for developing communication skills and greater self-awareness.

Dating is a partner activity, so the ability to effectively communicate with another person is also important to develop. Different skills are appropriate during different stages of the dating process. For example, the practice of taking a leadership role and being assertive about interests early in the courtship is different from the practice of learning about your date as a potential life partner. Both are completely different from the nonverbal communication that is also constantly occurring during a date. Understand your client's dating process and create exercises that focus on specific targets. Make

S.M.A.R.T. (Specific, Measurable, Actionable, Resonant, Time sensitive) goals that you can track and review with the clients as they build confidence.

Role-playing is a powerful tool the coach and client can make use of to improve communication and confidence. Take a situation the client fears and role-play it until it becomes mundane. Show clients that they are more than capable to handle the situation. Support them fumbling through the motions in the practice arena. The role-playing is a meaningful exercise which will give your clients confidence for the real life scenario when they approach it.

Visualization exercises are another great way for clients to increase their level of preparedness for a potentially vulnerable situation. Imagining intended outcomes, worst-case scenarios, and a few situations in between will give the client a sense of familiarity that will drive confidence.

MANAGING UNCERTAINTY

Dating involves a great deal of uncertainty. Clients are possibly wondering: Is she single? Will he find me attractive? What does she want? How do I ask him out? Is she committed? The list goes on and on. The sooner a client accepts that uncertainty is a natural, and even fun, part of the dating process, the closer they will be to achieving dating success. Instead of eliminating uncertainty, manage and embrace it.

> *"Instead of eliminating uncertainty, manage and embrace it."*

Master communicators possess and practice the skill of asking good questions. How does this make a difference? Questions are powerful communication tools. By asking genuinely curious questions and listening empathetically, you give your conversation partner the freedom to express him or herself. You invite vulnerability and thereby facilitate connection. This builds trust, demonstrates interest, and gives the gift of attention.

Miscommunication, like uncertainty, is a reality. New relationships are especially susceptible to it as you have very little background information and a low level of familiarity. A key skill to develop is asking clarifying questions. Two people can use the same words with completely different meanings. For example, the definition of a date, monogamy, or even love, can be drastically different from a date's understanding and usage of those words. The miscommunication fire is fueled by assuming you know what your partner means. Instead, practice with clients to ask for clarification. By encouraging feedback and thoughtful, expressive dialogue you will minimize miscommunication and set a framework of open connection.

161

OVERCOMING FEAR

Help clients to understand how fear impacts them. Ask how it shows up. For example it may be a physical sensation such as tension, or tightness. Alternatively it may affect energy levels or appetite. What does it do to their perspective? What reaction does it produce? Fear generates a biological signal. It creeps beyond the psychological. Animals can smell it. Create a habit of examining fear when it arises. Seek to understand what the body is communicating. Befriend fear. Meet the fear head on to move on your way toward managing it.

Instead of letting fear motivate actions, allow it to stimulate the mind. Once a fear is acknowledged and understood, it loses much of its influence over actions. This, in turn, makes you significantly more likely to achieve a better result.

What is the fear saying? What is causing discomfort? Often times my clients have told me grandiose apocalyptic narratives about the fear of rejection. These stories are built on the presupposition that rejection is a bad thing. How is that value judgment made?

The most successful professional relationship builders, a.k.a. salespeople, love rejection. How can this be? This is because rejection is a clear communication of priority or desire.

Someone who doesn't see your client as part of his or her vision for dating success likely will not be a fit for your client's vision of success. Thus, by clearly expressing their preference, he or she is doing the favor of not wasting your client's time. Knowing what doesn't work is an important part of finding out what does. Talk with your client about thanking them and moving on.

What is really driving a fear of rejection? Rejection is likely to occur very early in the dating process. Imagine if your client approaches a beautiful stranger. Feeling particularly brave, they directly state their intention, "Hi, I find you beautiful and want to take you on a date." Imagine this response, "I'm flattered, but I'm happily married, thank you." This is a rejection. Manageable, right? Too often, people build the prospect of rejection into a huge crush to the self-worth, one that will never be overcome. This is simply the result of fear mingling with imagination. A crushing impact is far from a likely or realistic outcome.

"Too often, people build the prospect of rejection into a huge crush to the self-worth, one that will never be overcome. This is simply the result of fear mingling with imagination. A crushing impact is far from a likely or realistic outcome."

Imagine a realistic worst-case scenario. How does its occurrence impact day-to-day life? How does it shift the future? Equipped with this knowledge, reconsider the best-case scenario: the date, the passion, the kiss, etc. Is it worth the risk of the worst-case scenario? What are the reasons?

The number one way to overcome fear is to face it head on with authentic action. Lean in. As a coach, identify exercises to help your client grow past fear. Remember, like training muscles, your clients can work consistently over time and get to the edge of their comfort zones. Empower them to take action, experience results, and build confidence. Eventually they will reach a point where the fear is effectively managed. This is when you've helped sculpt their courage 6-pack.

What some call uncertainty others call romance. It's a matter of perspective. Regardless of what your client's is, that perspective makes up half of the relationship's perspective. When two people meet and begin dating, even if there is physical attraction, intellectual compatibility, and personal warmth, there is no guarantee that the relationship will turn out the way either person intends.

Relationships are dynamic and constantly changing. The uncertainty can be extremely exciting and induce butterflies in the stomach. Or it can be debilitating. Perspective is the difference maker. If your client feels confident that they are communicating authentically and pursuing the emotional and relationship goals they have set for themselves, they will be excited to see the results and what comes next.

DATING IS FUN

Dating is meant to be enjoyed. Clearly define your client's vision of dating success. How do they want to feel? What does their ideal match look like? How does their ideal date treat them? How does their date or partner impact their life? Dig a level deeper beyond these answers and really understand what your client wants to get out of dating. In order to communicate these values and desires to another person, help your clients first develop a great understanding of self. There are many exercises to uncover this awareness. For example, survey friends and loved ones because these are the people most familiar with your client's virtues. Make a list. Celebrate these virtues. Remember to practice them often. This will create a powerful assurance of worthiness, which will propel pursuit of the relationship of your client's dreams.

"…help your clients first develop a great understanding of self."

Ask your client: What kind of people do you enjoy spending time with? What is your communication style? How do you want to feel? What will this relationship do for other areas of your life? Who attracts you? What do you want to build with someone? How do you want dating to fit into your life? What kinds of people enjoy spending time with you? These questions and many others will inform what and who to look for. Being able to communicate these desires effectively demonstrates confidence and invites a partner to share his or her authentic self and goals. This gives both people information to make intelligent decisions about the relationship.

THE GOLDEN RULE OF RELATIONSHIPS

You get what you give. It is critically important to know what and who you are looking for in a relationship. To win, know your definition of victory. A successful relationship or partnership of any kind is best built on both personal and altruistic motivation. For a relationship to prosper and sustain, both people must be better together than apart. There is interdependence inherent in every successful relationship. The more value each provides their partner, the better they become, and the more value they offer in return. A virtuous cycle is created. The same way your client has emotional and relationship goals so does their prospective partner.

Whether looking for a summer-time fling, casual dating, or a life partner, consider the other person in the relationship. They have goals and a vision for the kind of relationships they seek. Ask your client: How do you satisfy this vision? What value are you providing? How do you want your partner to feel? What do you want to give your partner? What kind of activities do you want to share with someone? How do you want to spend time with each other? What structure do you want to co-create for the relationship?

> *"Ask your client: How do you satisfy this vision?*
> *What value are you providing?"*

Dating is about fun, pleasure, and connection. Challenge your client to give those experiences to someone else and they will find a great deal of joy in their dating life.

FINAL THOUGHTS

Confidence is communicated by those who know their values and act with integrity towards them. Communication is the constant feedback loop through which people in a relationship evaluate relationship health. Many of the saboteurs of dating success, regardless of personal definition, stem from poor communication. Often poor communication results from fear or lack of self-understanding. These are both easy to overcome

167

with some targeted support. Coaching provides a structure to clarify personal values, improve communication of those values, and encourages action that drives results. This creates a great sense of confidence and worthiness that empowers an individual to go and achieve relationship success.

If you want to improve your results, seek coaching. Embrace the process. Life is short. Human connection is one of the most precious resources available. Go after what you want in a genuine way and do your best to authentically appreciate what you have in your relationships. Dating success is an opportunity.

"If you want to improve your results, seek coaching."

Michael Zaytsev is a Brooklyn based Entrepreneur, Community Organizer, and Coach. He organizes High NY, the largest network of Cannabis entrepreneurs and activists in New York. He is a facilitator for the TEDxNewYorkSalon team. Michael produces various events across New York City bringing diverse groups of people together around their common interest to create positive impact. He also mentors NYC startups and on sales and growth strategy.

After working in private wealth management for J.P. Morgan and enterprise sales for Google, Michael became a life and business coach. Passionate about human connection, tech innovation, and personal development, he is dedicated to helping others maximize their potential. He helps transform his clients' businesses or personal lives by creating spaces to freely explore their values and desires, facilitating a deeper connection to the individual's authentic self.

He holds a Bachelor's of Arts in Economics from Claremont McKenna College. He fell in love with public service and leadership while serving in student government at Stuyvesant High School. Michael loves sharing meals with his friends and family.

www.TheCoach.nyc

CHOOSING THE RIGHT LIFE PARTNER

Dr. Renée van Heerden

Imagine how awesome if fairy tales were true. In fairy tales a brave, handsome prince meets a stunningly beautiful princess and it is love at first sight. After he has captured her heart they live happily ever after! The reality is that the longest sentence in the world is, "I do!" Whether it is marriage or committing to a partner in a long-term relationship, starry-eyed couples soon enough discover the truth of this statement: Lasting love is both a matter of the heart and it is also a matter of the head.

The scenario that presents itself is all too familiar. Clients contact life coaches after a devastating breakdown of a relationship, mainly for two reasons: to assist them to pick up the pieces of their lives and get direction again and to establish the reason things went wrong in order to avoid repeating the same mistakes again.

Alternatively clients feel stuck in a life that is lonely and unfulfilling. Sometimes they lack the self-confidence and courage to brave it in unfamiliar territory and go out, meet people, and enter into a relationship. Their hope is that entering a coaching relationship will provide guidance.

The consequences of a broken relationship can be devastating.

Clients' self-image and confidence levels have often been seriously damaged. It may mean clients experience financial difficulty. They may be pushed to break ties with mutual friends and seek a new circle of friends; there may be doubt as to who their real friends are. New life styles have to be developed and it is difficult to know where to begin.

Choosing a suitable marriage/life partner is a very important decision, and worthy of thought. Throughout this chapter the fact that the choice of a life/marriage partner is both a matter of the heart and also a matter of the head will be emphasized and explained.

STARTING WITH THE CLIENT

A healthy relationship involves two people with different identities giving each other the space to retain their own identity whilst supporting each other to grow in his/her identity. This is possible only when the individuals have a clear understanding of their own identity, their own dreams, and their own aspirations for the future.

> *"A healthy relationship involves two people with different*
> *identities giving each other the space*
> *to retain their own identity whilst*
> *supporting each other to grow in his/her identity."*

The place to start the process of searching for a suitable marriage/life partner is with the client, instead of with the potential partner. This phase involves the question: "Who are you?" It is absolutely essential that clients arrive at self-awareness and a clear understanding of themselves. This involves exploring with them what makes up their core identity, their background history, and any areas that require healing (which may indicate counseling first before coaching), their strengths and challenges, and also what they want out of life. Without this insight clients will be unable to accurately assess the suitability of a potential partner because, without the necessary self-knowledge, they will be unable to recognise whether a potential partner is a good or bad match, and they will be unable to identify possible challenge areas.

> *"The place to start the process of searching for a suitable marriage/life partner is with the client..."*

People can be defined using many different categories such as race, culture, language, religion, sexual orientation, economic status, educational background, profession, personality traits, etc. The idea is that people belonging to a specific category will think, feel and behave in a certain way. We know that each person is unique! A more accurate statement is that clients tend to think, feel and behave according to what they consider to be their core identity, those aspects of their make-up that make them their own unique individual.   The critical consideration is which of these categories are particularly important to clients in describing themselves.   Individuals may fit into a particular category and for them it may or may not form an important part of their identity.

> *"...clients tend to think, feel and behave according to what they consider to be their core identity ..."*

Once clients have arrived at a clear picture of what they consider to be their core identity, those aspects of their make-up that most accurately describe who they are, it is vital that they gain an understanding of how their background history can have a profound influence on their relationships.   Perceptions about relationships are shaped by the relationship one's parents had with each other and also by personal experiences in previous relationships.   It is important for clients to identify whether there are unresolved, hurtful issues from the past that may influence future relationships, and if appropriate, enter into professional therapy for these areas before entering into a new relationship.

Because it is important for clients to have a realistic picture of who they are it is very useful to explore what they believe their strengths to be, as well as the areas they find challenging.   This is an area that is very subjective and very closely related to their

174

self-image and sense of self-worth. Often the coaching process includes considerable work with clients in this area to support a positive self-image. It is especially important that clients also identify their fears and reservations in terms of future relationships (e.g., that they will end up in an abusive relationship again) and that those fears are addressed.

Once the areas mentioned above are resolved, clients are ready to address the choice of a potential marriage/life partner.

REASONS FOR CHOOSING A MARRIAGE/LIFE PARTNER

"I should have seen the warning signs right from the start: we were just wrong for each other." These are words that life coaches hear far too often from clients. The question is, if these warning signs were present from the beginning of the relationship, what is the reason were they ignored? The answer is most often found in the underlying reasons the client committed to a particular marriage or life partner, or for committing to a longstanding relationship in the first place.

Upon exploring the reasons clients chose a particular marriage or life partner, life coaches may come across some of the following explanations:

- "There was a strong chemistry (physical attraction) between us"
- "I was desperately lonely"
- "I fancied the idea of marriage/a relationship, because I believed it would provide me with a sense of security and belonging"
- "I felt sorry for my partner"
- "I was so used to having my partner around, I could not imagine life without him/her and I mistook that for love"
- "I tried to get back at another person"
- "My parents and/or friends put pressure on me because they liked my partner so much"
- "My friends & family all warned me but, out of rebellion I wanted to prove to them they were wrong"
- "I was struggling financially and thought this would be a solution"
- "I wanted a father/mother for my kid"
- "In the back of my mind I had this picture of growing old on my own and I feared that, if I let go of this relationship, nobody else might be interested in me"
- "It was a good career decision'"

Unfortunately clients discover that none of these are good enough reasons for committing to a serious, long standing relationship without first considering a number of other very important factors.

CRITERIA FOR CHOOSING A MARRIAGE/LIFE PARTNER

In exploring with clients what it is that they want for their lives, life coaches will find it useful to get clients to consider the criteria they wish to apply in choosing a marriage/life partner.

The aspects for consideration before entering into a serious relationship are important because, if they are ignored, it is very likely that these aspects will become problematic at some stage of a relationship and, unfortunately, the couple will become part of the statistics.

There are a myriad of aspects that form part of the criteria that can be included in such a list.   Listed below are some essential considerations:

SIMILARITIES AND DIFFERENCES IN CORE IDENTITY

The importance for clients to identify the factors making up their own core identity was covered previously.   Of equal importance is to consider how similar or different this core identity is from that of the prospective partner.

It is entirely possible for people to have successful relationships despite significant differences.   Different does not mean wrong!

Differences can be complementary. In order to have a meaningful relationship, both partners have to be sure of what they consider to be their own core identity, and there must some shared common ground with the core identity of their marriage/life partner. Although differences may initially be seen as exciting and fascinating, they can also ultimately become a huge challenge in a relationship. These challenges are best considered beforehand and both parties can commit to being willing to make compromises. Some of the aspects to explore are:

- Similarities and differences in terms of race, cultural, and home language backgrounds
- Similarities and differences in terms of religious backgrounds
- Similarities and differences in terms of educational background and economic status
- Similarities and differences in terms of professions

The bigger the differences, the more potential room there is for misunderstandings, differences in opinions, conflict, and frustration. Therefore areas where there are significant differences are best discussed beforehand. The couple will want to come to an agreement regarding how these differences will be managed in their relationship.

> *"Therefore areas where there are significant differences are best discussed beforehand."*

SIMILARITIES AND DIFFERENCES IN AGE

The larger the age difference between prospective partners, the more understanding and adaption will be required by both of them. People in different life cycles tend to have different wants, life styles, and energy levels. Huge age differences may be interesting during the initial stages of the relationship, and may become problematic later.

SIMILARITIES AND DIFFERENCES IN BACKGROUNDS

The way in which individuals were brought up and the values they learned from their parents form an integral part of who they are as adults. While some people retain these values, others try their utmost to get as far away as possible from what they were exposed to in their backgrounds. The point to consider here is that, whatever the client's background, and that of their prospective partner, it will have an influence on their relationship. The more similar their home backgrounds, the greater mutual understanding and similarity in core values. It is important to remember that in a serious relationship or marriage clients enter into a relationship with both their partner and also with their partner's family. It is helpful, therefore, for clients to consider the relationship and anticipate potential conflict areas with their partners' relatives. It is also helpful for clients to consider whether there is a history in their own or their prospective partner's family lines of incurable, dreaded disease, psychiatric illness, patterns of abuse, addiction, etc. that they want to take into consideration.

> *"It is important to remember that in a serious relationship or marriage clients enter into a relationship with both their partner and also with their partner's family."*

After a break-up many couples can testify that their friends and family all tried to warn them before hand, but that they had chosen to ignore these warning signals, either because they were rebellious, or because they wanted to prove everyone wrong. It is wise for clients to remind themselves that loved ones have their best interest at heart and therefore ask themselves: "What do they see that I do not see?"

Once again, while successful relationships between parties coming from totally different home backgrounds are entirely possible, the challenges that will have to be overcome by huge differences in home backgrounds will have to be considered beforehand, and both parties have to be willing to make compromises. If both parties come from *'broken'* homes with a history of childhood trauma & abuse, both parties will have to realize that a significant amount of healing will first have to take place in order for the relationship to be stable and comfortable.

SIMILARITIES AND DIFFERENCES IN PERSONALITY

It is unusual that two people with exactly the same personality make-up and temperament will get along. Significant personality differences may also cause conflict. The aim is to work toward a situation where personality differences are identified, mutual understanding is created, and these differences are viewed as ways in which the parties complement each other.

SIMILARITIES AND DIFFERENCES IN COMMUNICATION STYLE

Differences in communication style may be a huge source of conflict in relationships. The basis of a successful relationship is good communication. Questions to be considered are:

- What value does each person place on communication within the relationship?
- What are the similarities and differences in core values?
- How will they make time for communication?
- How does respect for each other support the basis of communication between the parties?
- How are differences communicated?
- How is conflict managed and resolved?
- How is love communicated?
- How willing and committed to working on the relationship is each person?

181

WHAT IS THE LEVEL OF TRUST AND INTEGRITY?

A lack of trust in the relationship will make it very difficult to experience a sense of safety and security.   An important question to consider is whether one or both of the people involved have trust issues from the past to be addressed.   In doing so potential conflict in the relationship will be minimized and a sense of safety in the relationship will be created.

WHAT IS THE LEVEL OF UNDERSTANDING AND SUPPORT?

Many jokes have been made about the 'for better or for worse' clause in the marriage vows.   The reality is that any relationship experiences times of sunshine and also times of rain. Clients will want to consider whether their prospective partners will be available for them during the times of rain to offer empathy, support, and understanding.

SIMILARITIES AND DIFFERENCES IN HABITS AND INTERESTS

A common saying has it that opposites attract.   This might be true in dating; in long-term relationships differences in habits can become irritating and a source of conflict.   Major differences in interests, on the other hand, may lead to a relationship with either two people drifting apart or one of the partners having to sacrifice their interests completely, ultimately feeling very unfulfilled. Each person is unique. Two people with exactly the same interests and habits may find life becomes monotonous. What is important is that similarities and differences in habits and interests be identified and discussed beforehand. The aim is for two people to complement each other in their differences.

> *"The aim is for two people to*
> *complement each other in their differences."*

THE IMPORTANCE OF SETTING HEALTHY BOUNDARIES

Although some people view boundaries as restricting rules, successful relationships require healthy boundaries. What are boundaries? Boundaries in relationships can be described as guidelines or limits people set for themselves in terms of what are considered permissible ways for other people to behave, and what is unacceptable. Boundaries that are healthy in a relationship provide safety and security plus it serves to preserve the each person's identity. It is healthy for clients to identify their own boundaries and also those of their prospective partner. If one of them tends to demand constant attention, validation, and re-assurance from the other the importance of setting healthy boundaries to retain an individual sense of identity becomes even more crucial.

Clients may also want to identify relationship deal breakers very early in their relationship. Deal breakers are aspects considered to be absolutely unacceptable in the relationship, and which provide sufficient justification to one of the parties for ending the relationship. Examples of deal breakers include abuse (physical, sexual, emotional, or verbal), infidelity, addiction (, substance, gambling, or sexual addiction), and sometimes even include things such as having children or no children, or pets or no pets.

Two people enter a relationship, each with their own boundaries (or lack of boundaries). While it is important that the boundaries of each one be identified, these boundaries can be re-negotiated as the relationship develops and provides more safety and security.

SIMILARITIES AND DIFFERENCES IN PREFERRED LIFESTYLE

During the initial stages of a relationship people are in love and tend to overlook major differences in preferred life style. Then, sometimes, conflict erupts about differences in terms of where they want to live, how they wish to spend their free time and holidays, who their friends are, how often they socialize with friends, or how they manages their time. These are all factors better considered beforehand. The client ideally engages in open and honest discussion with a prospective partner about each other's preferred life style and in this way they will also get to know each other better.

> *"The client ideally engages in open and honest discussion with a prospective partner..."*

SIMILARITIES AND DIFFERENCES IN CAREERS

Clients are asked to consider the similarities and differences between their own career and that of their prospective partner. How compatible are their views about their careers? Or, perhaps even more important, is the major attraction to this person more a case of a business decision than real love?

SIMILARITIES AND DIFFERENCES IN DESIRING PARENTHOOD AND IN RAISING CHILDREN

It is important for prospective partners to establish beforehand whether they actually want the same thing. What is their interest in having children? If they do have children, what are

185

their views on parenting in terms of maintaining discipline, parental involvement, and nurturing respect for each other within the family?   What are the specific fears and concerns in terms of parenting to be addressed?   In many instances an additional factor to be considered is whether the client or their prospective partner already have children of their own.   How does this influence the relationship?   What kind of father/mother will the prospective partner be to their children? Even more complicated are dealing with an ex-spouse/partner, children's visitation arrangements, and disciplining the other's children.   The client will be well served to discuss all of this extensively beforehand.

SIMILARITIES AND DIFFERENCES IN MANAGING FINANCES

Differences in how finances are managed can cause a huge amount of conflict and it is essential that the individuals come to some form of an agreement on how they, as a couple, wish to manage their finances.   Consideration will be given as to what their expectations are of each other in terms of providing an income and contributing to the household finances.   Reaching an agreement on financial management in cases where financial commitments exist in terms of ex-spouses/partners and/or children can be complicated so give serious consideration to these very important areas.

Arriving at useful answers to the above questions requires courage and complete honesty. A coach can facilitate honesty from clients by creating a safe, non-judgmental environment where clients feel free to explore, and also by explaining to clients that, without this honesty, they are limiting themselves in terms of the benefits from the coaching process. This might be a painful process; it is less than the future pain it will prevent.

> *"A coach can facilitate honesty from clients*
> *by creating a safe, non-judgmental environment*
> *where clients feel free to explore…"*

ACTION PLANNING FOR MEETING AND CHOOSING A POTENTIAL PARTNER

Instead of fixed recipes when it comes to coaching prepare with helpful guidelines. When it comes to choosing a suitable marriage/life partner each client's circumstances will be unique. During the coaching process life coaches, serving as strategic partners, equip clients to give careful consideration to critical aspects in choosing a potential marriage/life partner. This can be a highly emotional process for clients, especially when it comes to self-awareness and facing realities that they have been avoiding. Clients may even resist talking about or addressing certain aspects, or give what they believe to be the desired responses. While remaining extremely supportive all the time,

187

life coaches will find it appropriate to respectfully confront their clients at times.

It is important for clients' expectations of the coaching process to be clarified beforehand to avoid unrealistic expectations of the coach actually helping them to make a choice or making choices for them.

The success of the coaching process will largely depend on how honest clients are prepared to be about themselves to address their own vulnerabilities. For this to take place the coaching environment will have to be one of safety and support.

> *"The success of the coaching process will largely depend on how honest clients are prepared to be about themselves to address their own vulnerabilities."*

Once clients have given careful consideration to the criteria discussed above, an action plan can be devised. The section below is intended to serve as a helpful guideline.

CREATING SELF-AWARENESS

Clients, with the help of the coach, are well served to arrive at a level of self-awareness where they understand who they are, what their core identity is, what their strengths are, and also

188

what their challenges are or areas that can be developed. Having a high level of self awareness is an important aspect of emotional maturity and of developing one's Emotional Intelligence (the ability to manage emotions intelligently). This in turn supports a stable and satisfying relationship.

> *"Having a high level of self-awareness is an important aspect of emotional maturity and of developing one's Emotional Intelligence."*

DEVELOPING THE CLIENT'S SELF-ESTEEM

Before any constructive work can be done in terms of finding or choosing a suitable marriage or life partner, it might be appropriate for life coaches to address self-esteem with clients. The choice of a marriage/life partner is largely dependent on how much clients value themselves.

Often clients who have experienced severe rejection and long periods of loneliness tend to struggle with cultivating a more positive outlook on life and can benefit from the assistance of the coach in this area. Instead of approaching this journey with anxiety and reservation, clients will be encouraged to instead approach this as an exciting, fun-filled journey. Venturing out and taking calculated risks can be done appropriately with the support and encouragement of the coach.

189

CREATING A WISH LIST

It is sometimes useful for clients to draw up a wish list in terms of what they are ideally looking for in a partner. This wish list is flexible and serves as a well-considered guideline for choosing a partner. It is important that this wish list be realistic. This wish list is used only as a guideline, summarising the ideal attributes of a prospective partner.

WHERE TO MEET A PROSPECTIVE PARTNER?

Life often throws unexpected surprises at us, and one might meet a potential partner at an unexpected place. If clients have clarity of what they are looking for in a potential partner, it makes sense to ask a very practical question: Where are you likely to meet such a person?

CREATING A TIME LINE

It is impossible to set a concrete time line for meeting a suitable prospective partner. It often happens unexpectedly, which makes it all the more exciting. It is possible to set a time line for being prepared if the right person happens to appear. Clients can be encouraged to set realistic time lines for areas of self-development, for taking on new, exciting activities, for sorting out challenging areas in their lives, etc. It is critical that clients understand the importance that actively working on self-improvement is a life-long journey, and more than for the purpose of finding a suitable marriage/life partner.

CONCLUSION

There are a myriad of aspects that form part of the criteria to be included in choosing a suitable marriage/life partner, and the areas listed above are some of the important ones to be considered.

The premise for this chapter is that love is both a matter of the heart and also a matter of the head. In choosing a suitable marriage/life partner matters of the heart are extremely important. When it comes to such an important, life-changing decision, it is equally important to be rational and practical.

As life/relationship coaches, we want our clients to find that fairytale relationships and yes, happily-ever-after endings actually do come true. The journey in getting there is different than described in the classical fairytale. It is about cultivating opportunity and such a relationship. Clients will come to the understanding that the work continues once they enter into a relationship; that is when the actual work begins! The coach can assist clients in this by helping them to explore ways they will facilitate continuous growth in their relationship.

What is missing in the fairytale is that the initial sprinkle of fairy dust tends to settle after some time. It is after the fairy dust has settled that, if the initial choice was accompanied by a measure of rational, calculated decision-making, as well as a commitment by both parties to continuously put work and effort in sustaining the relationship, the couple becomes a team and there will be a good prognosis for the desired happily-ever-after outcome.

> *"It is after the fairy dust has settled that, if ...*
> *the couple becomes a team and there will be a good prognosis*
> *for the desired happily-ever-after outcome."*

Renee van Heerden lives in South Africa and specializes as a consultant implementing Trauma Management programs in organizations, Trauma Counseling, Grief Counseling, On-the-Scene Trauma, and Life Coaching.

Renee is an EMDR practitioner and Certified Master Coach offering training in Life Skills Development and the development of Emotional Intelligence. She offers awareness sessions on dealing with Trauma, Grief, and life skills related issues. Renee is a motivational speaker.

Renee holds a D Lit. ET Phil in Research Psychology, an honors degree in Communication, and a BA Ministry Degree in Christian Counseling. She is a trained ambulance worker.

Renee offers 6 years of experience as a Human Resources manager at a large, international organization and 10 years as a senior researcher at a research institute.

As part of her life skills development program, Renee has a special interest in the development of women and in assisting couples to establish healthy and sound relationships.

As a motivational speaker Renee regularly presents on Trauma Awareness, Life Skills, and couple relationship related topics.

Transition Coaching
Meg Hanrahan

Change is the only constant, as the old saying goes. We know from life experience with many shifts and twists, forks and turns, that this is true. For all its commonality, change is often challenging. It's to be expected then that as coaches we find clients are undergoing change.

The change may be welcome, of a person's choosing, bringing joy. Other times it is an intruder, an unwelcome visitor who comes knocking at the door. It might relate to career, a change of position or jobs, a promotion or demotion. It might be family status, a marriage or divorce, the birth of children, children leaving home, or the death of a loved one. Alternatively it may revolve around health, perhaps brought on by injury, illness, or aging. Overall change relates to transition through the natural stages of life.

> *"Overall change relates to transition through the natural stages of life."*

CHANGE AND TRANSITION

Whatever the individual circumstances of transition, there are similarities to the process and concepts that help a person move gracefully and grow with the change. Understanding the

195

dynamics of this powerful process helps a coach offer effective support during these important times in a person's life.

So, what exactly is transition?   Defined as a movement, development, or evolution from one form or stage to another, transition includes three stages:

- Separating or letting go
- Waiting, sometimes called the neutral zone
- Re-entry and transformation into something new

The order depicts the general direction and trend of growth, and stages generally overlap.   All three stages are commonly experienced and the order varies.

It's obvious that transition involves change; transition and change are sometimes accepted as synonymous.   Transition is the process of personal development that often accompanies change, a process whereby we grow and transform.   By way of contrast, it's possible to experience change in life without being notably altered by it.   Transition is a deeper level of change, a type of change that involves more than an outward set of circumstances; transition is a catalyst that has the potential to transform a person's life inside and out.

It's often most helpful to see the process of transition as a pilgrimage or journey.   Journeys have many ups and downs,

196

starts and stops, periods of being on track, of being lost, and of re-routing.

How do coaches support clients through these various stages of change?   What can we do to help clients embrace new avenues of possibility?   How do we help them stay on track and find fortitude to make it successfully across the chasm to the next cycle of growth?

Exploring the stages of transition provides a good basis for understanding the entire process more fully.

LETTING GO

We all benefit from the ability to let go with ease; it's a goal to which we aspire.   Many people find that releasing the past, letting go of what has been or what is no longer working for them, is a challenge.   It can be hard to let go of what we know, whether what we have known has been experienced as positive or negative.   Coaches provide instrumental support during this early stage.

Remember that the definition of transition suggests progress and we are trained as coaches to help clients structure goals and move toward what they do want.   Coaches maintain this

197

emphasis: looking toward growth, toward dreams and goals, toward the next stage.

> *"Coaches maintain this emphasis: looking toward growth, toward dreams and goals, toward the next stage."*

How do we maintain forward focus while satisfying the interests of the client in an activity that naturally relates back to something? How does letting go fit with the process of transition? Which type of professional support is best?

Letting go is a natural part of the cycle of growth. We look around us to know this is true. Trees drop their leaves in the fall, a process that makes way for the emergence of new leaves in spring. Snakes shed their skins in order to grow new ones. Baby birds leave the safety of the nest in order to spread their wings and fly. We are the same. We let go to move forward. In reciprocal fashion, it is in looking out and stretching forward that we find the courage to let go and leap.

When we find ourselves in the peculiar environment wrought by change in our lives, the experience does provide a unique opportunity for engaging with the past, good, bad, ugly, or beautiful. This process is normal and often healthy. It's a process that often stimulates personal and creative development to motivate the forward progress that is our goal.

Soul searching, whereby we ask the timeless question, "Who am I?" is a common hallmark of the transition process. There is a desire to discover the self anew and an opportunity to reinvent oneself; that desire and opportunity often develop out of the urge to release an old identity and step into the new.

We help clients find balance amid these dynamics by recognizing that we are in a process that is moving forward even as we take time to reflect on the past. Additionally, we support clients in letting go by encouraging cultivation of specific attitudes:

- Attitudes of willingness - willingness to let go, willingness to experience change and transformation, willingness to embrace the journey.
- Attitudes of compassion - especially compassion for self as they leave the territory of the familiar and walk into the unknown, an experience that often produces feelings of apprehension or loss.

It is encouraging to watch someone move through this transition when progressing in a positive way. What do we do if a client does get bogged down? Here are a couple of techniques:

- Body scanning: a process whereby we simply breathe into and witness the sensations in our body; it is a powerful and gentle way to assist us in letting go to move forward. Ask the client to pay attention to their breathing and to notice what's going on in the body while maintaining the breath. Then pose follow-up questions: What are you feeling? Where are you feeling it? What is it saying to you?

- Focus on the positive: ask the client to visualize the completion of a goal. Then help extend and enrich the positive experience, engaging all of the senses, by asking: What do you see? Hear? Feel? Smell? Taste? Filling the body with the positive experience the client is warmed by the fire of what has been imagined. This process stimulates forward progress.

WAITING THEN CROSSING THE CHASM

Life transitions usually include a period of uncertainty, a time of waiting, a neutral zone. There is often a sense of searching while sometimes what, exactly, we're searching for is unclear. There's a sense of waiting; waiting for what? Our vision of the future may be obscured. We are wanderers in a wilderness of uncertainty.

We're unaccustomed to this ebbing of the tide. It may feel like a wanted rest for some. More often it's perceived as uncomfortable, especially in western cultures. It's common to feel this time of waiting as emptiness, and emptiness as loss.

Additionally there's discomfort because we are unsure how long this period will last. Moving through the neutral zone with all of its uncertainty takes time, an undetermined amount of time. However long it takes, it may feel too long.

Coaches help clients through feelings of discomfort by exploring this as a stage. Traveling through an unknown landscape is part of the natural cycle of transition. The tide will come in again. Spring will come after the long and hard winter. Activity will follow periods of rest as we wait for the future to make itself known.

People undergoing the second stage of transition value reassurance and encouragement to trust in their own inner resources.

> *"People undergoing the second stage of transition value reassurance and encouragement to trust in their own inner resources."*

Challenging times such as these are common on the transformational journey. It takes a lot of courage to follow life's path to the abyss of the unknown, to approach the edge of our uncertainty, and to jump. We're rewarded for our courage when we cross the chasm to a new start.

Coaches support clients through this middle phase of transition by brainstorming with them to discover tools such as:

- Meditation, mindfulness, and/or prayer
- Conscious acceptance of uncertainty
- Journaling through the experience
- Cultivation of solitude and quiet
- Trust in the process

LEADING WITH THE HEART

One of the outcomes of the middle phase is learning that we can trust the quiet voice and mind of our own intuition. We learn to experience life simply and directly. We learn to lead with the heart, with our inner knowing.

How do we get from here to there? How do we know we're making the right choice? How do we know which way to go? Consider the power of the heart to guide.

We see that the heart is a key element in the intuitive process. During transition, intuition or being led by the heart acts as our compass steering us in the direction of our potential and growth.

It is important for the coach to hold to the truth that, whatever the circumstances, the client has the answers within. There may be many stops and starts; the path with heart will make

202

itself known.   When the client is ready, the opportunity comes.

> *"It is important for the coach to hold to the truth that,*
> *whatever the circumstances,*
> *the client has the answers within."*

We might call this process finding heart coherence.   Remember, the heart knows which way to go.   We can trust the client to know how to let go, how to find comfort, where to find support, and which paths to follow.

Tips for helping clients:
- Support small risk-taking to enter new territories.
- Build on small successes.

FINDING AND CHOOSING OPTIONS

If a client is moving forward in the process of transitioning there will come a time when they are ready to embrace change and look to new areas of growth.   Coaches use a variety of tools to assist clients in finding, evaluating, and choosing options.

We generally begin the coaching relationship by asking the question, "What do you want?"   Put another way, we might ask, "How do you want to grow?"   Helping clients connect with their

203

urge to grow brings energy during times of transition.

These questions can feel very big. Two common considerations arise when coaches present them. Some people are challenged to feel inspired in any direction. "I don't know," is a common answer. Sometimes the client lacks enthusiasm, motivation, and / or clarity to proceed. If this is the case it's possible the client still has work to do with letting go or is still in the waiting phase. If other indications show readiness to move on the coach can help the client discover a path with heart.

It's often easy for clients to share what they *don't* want:

- I don't want to do that work anymore.
- I don't want to be overweight.
- I don't want to be bored.

When the client voices what they don't want quickly follow up by asking them to flip it into what they *do* want. This often results in a pause and it's important to allow plenty of time to explore what comes up. After discussion, reinforce the motto taught in coach training: *Do say what you do want.*

Follow-up questions can also be helpful in stimulating new ways of thinking when a client answers, "I don't know." Ask: "What *do* you know?" and, again from coach training, "If you did know, what is it?" Or, ask the client to describe someone they admire and then ask, "What would that person say?" Encourage them to explore and expand possibilities. There are a lot of ways to do this. One way is to experiment with something completely new and different.

In corporations where innovation is the number one goal companies design spaces so that people from different departments run into each other because they know that they expand the possibility for innovation by connecting diverse people and ideas. In the same way doing something new, taking a class, meeting different people, or playing with different materials and processes are all things that help to generate new areas of growth.

Alternately, it sometimes helps to experience quiet time, solitude, and space to engage our intuition. Getting in tune with where we are when inspiration strikes will also help in finding heart-led guidance and answers. Inspiration, direction, and solutions often come in moments when we're relaxed and distracted, when we're not looking for them. Whether in the shower, driving, or taking a walk, it takes practice to pay attention and catch the guidance.

Encourage the client to notice where they are when ideas come to them and to find a committed manner for recording ideas. Keeping a journal is worthwhile for people in transition.

There are many other activities that stimulate a client's growth and promote heart coherence during this pilgrimage. Encourage them to use one or more of the following techniques:

- Engage the right brain. Brainstorm new and different ideas with a technique called mind mapping.

- Dialogue with your future self to get ideas and find answers. This process provides insight by connecting clients with their deeper knowing. Use it as a method in conjunction with regular journaling.

> *"Dialogue with your future self*
> *to get ideas and find answers."*

- Pay attention to signals. Notice coincidences and synchronicities. Synchronicity is the experience of things that are sometimes unrelated happening together in a meaningful way.

- Explore dreams. Ask: What are your dreams? What have you wanted to do? What did you love to do as a child that you want to do again? What do you want to do if money was no object and your success was assured?

- Follow your gut. This is a good practice for making decisions. What does it tell you to do?

- Follow your courage. Ask: What are you afraid to do? What would you do if you weren't afraid? Where does your courage lead?

- Encourage a willingness to fail, the practice of being uncomfortable, and the practice of taking risks.

Some people have so many ideas that they are unsure of which way to turn. For clients such as this it's like standing at a crossroads with opportunities and temptations calling in every direction. Making a choice among so many options is the challenge. If that's the case help the client focus attention using active judgment to make choices and take action. Some specific strategies include:

- Decide to start somewhere. Do something. Get out of your head and into action. Doing something frees energy to stimulate forward progress and development.

- Categorize ideas into imaginary keep, throw away, and store piles, then prioritize everything in the keep pile. This strategy helps identify the direction that holds the most energy.

- Remind clients that they have everything it takes to find clarity. Encourage them to connect with their inner knowing. The encouragement is sometimes all it takes.

DISCOVERING RESOURCES

Every living organism uses resources to grow. We use resources to help us grow toward our goals and dreams. People who are in transition, as they feel their ground shifting and the chasm of transformation widening, value having ample resources and areas of support. Coaches play a key role in helping clients discover sources for support.

Resources, like natural resources, sometimes require excavation to be found. This is especially true when it comes to personal strengths and skills. For some reason we're often out of touch with the means for support that is closest, what resides within. We discover, once we go digging, that there is a great breadth and depth of resourcefulness and strength inside.

> *"We discover, once we go digging, that there is a great breadth and depth of resourcefulness and strength inside."*

We help clients discover their deeper resources by providing encouragement to mine what is below the surface. Ask: When was another time in your life when you used strength from within? What personal resources did you find and use then? Personal strengths and resources to explore include:

- Emotional resources and strengths. Help the client connect with the emotional resources that have been instrumental in getting them to this stage of life or point of change. Having engaged in the reflective aspects of transition an awareness of emotional strengths may be more apparent. Perhaps curiosity prompted them along or courage helped them leap. Maybe faith kept them moving forward despite challenges or they discovered compassion for self and others. Ask questions that prompt the client to discover emotional resources they have developed and can count on to help them now and in the future.

- Physical resources and strengths. It's easy to overlook health as a strength until we're without it. The same is true of many other aspects of our physicality; we take them for granted. Consider with your client the benefits of simple physical energy to help move through the three stages of transition. How do energy, health, and fitness support the direction of growth?

- Experience and education. It is gratifying to really appreciate the experience and education you've amassed in your life from birth through childhood, adolescence, into adulthood, and beyond. For someone making a life change taking a few moments (or hours or days) to appreciate the vastness of life experiences that have been amassed, and appreciating those experiences as teachers, is a worthwhile exercise. It can take many forms: creating a list, compiling a CV (curriculum vitae), journaling, or writing a memoir are all worthwhile ways to find the value in our life experience. This, in turn, helps connect us with areas of strength and often results in a fresh sense of purpose.

- Mission, values, and legacy. Many people go day to day and year to year without identifying what is most important to them. Times of transition are especially ripe for thinking about mission and values along with the legacy that we want to create. In the midst of change considering the reasons we are here, what we most value, and what we want to accomplish over the course of our lives acts as a homing signal to meaningful growth in the future. Mission and values statements can act as mantras on our paths with heart. They help with decision-making and are guideposts that keep us on track as we traverse new territories of thought and action. Ask clients who have already formulated their mission, values, and legacy in writing how these can be added to the internal resources they already possess. Encourage others to take the time to engage in this potentially life-changing process.

The exploration of personal strengths and resources can become a touchstone in your work with clients in transition. In tandem, take time to discover external sources of support. Ask clients: Who supports you? What external resources do you have? External resources may include:

- Individual people
- Groups and networks
- Organizational partners

- Communities
- Classes
- Online resources
- Books
- Videos

Helping clients uncover their personal strengths and the resources that already exist, within and without, is gratifying. Keep going! The world is absolutely brimming with possibility. Follow up by asking: What resources do you want? Having done the work to uncover and appreciate the resources and strengths that already exist, clients feel empowered. They have a clear sense of direction and often find it easy to identify additional resources they want to acquire.

TRAVELING TIPS

In the back of many travel guides there is a section that provides tips for safe and happy journeys. This section is like that. People who have traversed the three stages of transition offer a variety of tips that may be helpful to others on their pilgrimage. Transition coaches, like travel agents, encourage clients to become aware of strategies that may make journeying more successful. Ask questions that stimulate consideration of the following:

- Pace: We all have an internal rhythm to which we feel most in tune with life. How happy are you with your current pace? What's your ideal pace?

- Patience: Transitions take time; many aspects are temporary. How does your experience of time impact your ability to move forward with ease?

- Professional Help: What support do you want from other professionals at this time? For example: a therapist, attorney, physician, or financial planner.

- Companions: Friends, family members, and colleagues can all act as companions on your journey. Who offers the kind of companionship that you want and that feels good? Who inspires you?

- Holistic Health: How do you take care of yourself? How will you nurture yourself even more? For example: relaxation, exercise, massage, yoga, or tai chi.

- Creativity and Play: Creative outlets and play are rewarding, especially if you're going through deep levels of change. What are you doing to express yourself and to have fun? How do you want to play and create?

- Nature: Many pilgrims consider nature a powerful, healing presence. Experiencing time walking, hiking, gardening, or just sitting in outdoor spaces can be restorative. How are you engaged by natural spaces and outdoor activities? Where is your healing space?

- Music: Music transcends words and speaks directly to the heart. What's the sound track of this time in your life? What is it saying to you?

- Journaling and Other Writing: Many poets are born out of life's transitions. Keeping a journal or writing poems, a memoir, or short stories during this special time can be both comforting and rewarding. What do you want to write about?

- Prayer and Other Spiritual Practices: Spiritual practices, the most common of which is prayer, are an important source of comfort and strength for many people. How is spirituality meaningful for you? What spiritual practices do you engage in? What type of spiritual experiences, if any, do you want?

- Meditation, Silence, and Rituals: Practices like meditation, silence, and rituals of many types are additional modalities that many people find meaningful. Meditation has been shown to have numerous benefits including physiological ones. How is the practice of meditation or silence meaningful to you? What practices support you on your way?

- Visualization: Visualization is a powerful technique for creating the life we want and can be used at any stage of transition. Recorded affirmations are one way we use this technique. How are you benefitting from your

213

recorded affirmations? What are some other ways to take advantage of this powerful practice?

- Travel: Making your way through major or minor life transitions is a journey. It makes sense then that actual travel often feels especially appropriate at this time. Where do you want to go?

We've all gained practical knowledge from our journeys through life's transitions. Gather additional tips you have gleaned along the way and add them to your travel guide. Consider additional questions to bring client awareness to personal and unique strategies for walking transition's road.

SUMMARY

Transition may touch any aspect of life: career, relationship, family, health, and normal life stages. It's more than change, it's a process whereby we grow and develop through change. While an individual's experience of transition is unique there are patterns that help us understand the process.

We can view transition as a journey through three main stages: letting go, waiting, and transitioning to something new. Letting go is a natural part of the process that is aided by willingness and self-compassion. Waiting is a period of uncertainty that requires trust in the process. Finally, transforming to something new occurs by following the path with heart.

> *"Finally, transforming to something new occurs by following the path with heart."*

There are many practical approaches to help clients move through the three stages of transition comfortably. A key task during this time is to find and choose options. Another is to discover personal resources, including emotional and physical strengths, experience and education, and mission and values. Finding external resources is helpful as well.

Most importantly, we as coaches trust clients to realize their own answers as they find and follow paths with heart. As we focus on the magnitude of the heart's ability to provide guidance we are on the right track. Traversing the journey that is transition we are most notably guided by remembrance of a simple maxim: the heart knows the way.

Meg Hanrahan is an award winning filmmaker, writer, and a committed coach. She works from a mission to inspire others toward deeper connections and positive change. Her programs and writings focus on personal well-being, evoke tolerance and understanding, and champion nature.

Meg has been providing services as a media producer, director, and writer through her company, Megrahan Media, since 1988. In 2013 Meg became certified as a professional coach through the Center for Coaching Certification. She specializes in life purpose, transition, and creativity coaching.

Meg offers workshops and provides special support to artists, writers, filmmakers, entrepreneurs, and others seeking to fulfill their creative goals through ArtLife Coaching & Training, a business launched in 2012.

Meg is a contributing author to the book *What Does God Look Like In An Expanding Universe?* (ImagoEarth Publishing, 2006) and is a longtime participant in Women Writing for a Change. She extends her reach in the community as Vice President and Trustee of Voyageur Media Group, Inc., a nonprofit whose mission is to create media about science, history, and culture. Meg is adjunct faculty at the University of Cincinnati Blue Ash in the Electronic Media Department.

VULNERABILITY IN LEADERSHIP
Marie Snidow

Ever play the child's game dodge ball? As a kid, did you ever grab the ball and with all of your might throw it at the nearest kid, thus eliminating them from the competition? In dodge ball, you have to be tough and fast. The winner is the kid who is able to move fast enough to avoid being hit by the ball while being aggressive enough to get others eliminated. If you get hit by the ball, you act like it didn't hurt. If your coaching clients are leaders today in business for themselves or in corporate America, they might ask, "What has really changed?"

If they are like many leaders, they've learned about leadership by watching other leaders in more senior positions. They read books about leadership or watch movies showing leaders in action such as Winston Churchill, Margaret Thatcher, Steve Jobs, and General George Patton.

As leaders, we learn to be tough minded, decisive, aggressive, results-oriented, and strong. We seek to become leader-like. Just as in our childhood dodge ball game we learn to stand tough, move fast, and never, ever appear vulnerable.

While leaders can be afraid to show vulnerability with staff members and in their organizations, in specific situations, it can be the very thing that makes the difference between good leadership and powerful, transformational leadership.

This chapter explores situations where leaders often feel vulnerable, risks that can be associated with clients using vulnerable behaviors on the job, strategies an executive coach can explore or brainstorm, and the surprising favorable outcomes that can occur.

If you are ready to help your coaching clients take their business and career to the next level and to challenge them in their growth as a leader, read on!

VULNERABILITY CONTRIBUTES TO GROWTH AND SUCCESS

The whole notion of vulnerability is an important one to explore because our human identity, the ego, and the very nature of the ego structure, is to defend or protect us.   The word vulnerability comes from the Latin word vulnus meaning wound.   Vulnerability is the state of being open to injury, undefended, and unshielded.   In Roman days, soldiers wore protective armor.   If some part of their body wasn't covered they were open to injury.   How many times as coaches do we guide our clients through many trials and circumstances where they are confronted with being or feeling open to injury?

Executive coaches must be skilled at recognizing situations where their clients can feel vulnerable, employing strategies that can help them access and show vulnerability, assessing the systems in which clients are operating and risk factors to consider, and recognizing powerful outcomes that can occur as a result.

There are many situations that occur in which clients feel vulnerable: an entrepreneur starting their own company, taking responsibility for something that went wrong at work, approaching work and superiors after a major setback, being promoted into a larger, more expansive role, or in building relationships with colleagues.

Two of the most common areas where vulnerability occurs are when leaders are promoted to a higher level role and when they choose to appear more open emotionally with others to build connection and trust.

> *"... common areas where vulnerability occurs are when leaders are promoted to a higher level role and when they choose to appear more open emotionally with others to build connection and trust."*

Whether promoted into a new job with broader responsibility or as a self-employed entrepreneur, executives are often required to take on a broader, more complex set of responsibilities. Due to the expansion of role and responsibilities, executives may feel pressure from their boss, direct reports, their organization and/or themselves to be the expert. Often times, executives have gotten to where they are in their career by developing and applying expert knowledge on the job. Then, as they move into more complex, expansive, and global roles, their sphere of influence increases significantly. They find that they cannot be the expert any more or rely on the expert model to lead effectively. This is a very big place of vulnerability for leaders because skills, knowledge, and tactics they have leaned on previously to get to where they are may be less effective now.

How often do leaders believe they are in their position because of their expertise? This way of thinking limits their ability to delegate and yes, empower others to effectively build a team. This calls for vulnerability with colleagues.

Organizations recognize the importance and value of grooming leaders who think more broadly about the business. Many global companies create rotation programs to move leaders strategically into different lines of business to help broaden their knowledge of the company and to expose them to larger business and organizational challenges. For example, a leader in manufacturing engineering with an electrical engineering degree and a staff of 200 is asked to rotate to lead the procurement or sales function for several years. This is designed to gain both a better perspective about those

221

departments and to align the procurement or sales function with manufacturing engineering. The results are an integrated, highly functioning department with the out of the box thinking the manufacturing engineer brings to the other functions. While this experience is valuable for both the leader and the organization, it can be stressful for the leader who wants to achieve success and also fears they cannot rely on their own functional expertise to get there.

While the last example pertains to a leader feeling vulnerable in a system or organizational setting, there is another situation leaders experience that might be harder to grasp and to coach: when leaders feel vulnerable as a person, emotionally or personally, in service of their leadership.

As coaches, we know the value of modeling vulnerability with our clients because it deepens our relationship, builds trust, and encourages sharing. A leader's relationships with their counterparts are the same. Leaders will be confronted with situations when they will benefit by sharing that they don't know how to do something, that they made a miscalculation about the strength of the competitor's product, or simply share more about themselves and their own struggles with their staff or colleagues. Addressing each of these opportunities supports leaders to be vulnerable, to take actions free of their armor, and to stay open to the outcomes.

EVALUATE RISK AND SYSTEMS

Coaches are responsible for being aware of and helping their clients explore the possible risks involved in being vulnerable and authentic within their organizations. Coaching a client to be vulnerable for vulnerability's sake is ineffective and irresponsible. When there is a reason for vulnerability with an expected outcome that will help clients achieve their goals and the vision of leadership into which they are growing, then coaching for vulnerability works.

> *"Coaches are responsible for being aware of and helping their clients explore the possible risks involved in being vulnerable and authentic within their organizations."*

Coaches first consider the organizational system in which the executive operates. Vulnerability in leadership may be counter-productive in certain aggressive kill or be killed cultures. Exploring vulnerability with clients may mean that they find, in order to be authentic, they want something other than an identity as a corporate person.

Coaches also explore a clients' openness to experimenting with vulnerability and their emotional agility for it. If they have been fighting since middle school to be the dodgeball winner, developing a thick skin, taking the knocks and getting back up, the expressions of identity are contrary to vulnerability and if vulnerability makes sense then a slower, more gradual approach may be best.

POSSIBLE STRATEGIES

When clients are faced with these new challenges, coaches employ a number of strategies to help them build courage to move into the space of vulnerability.

An executive coach I spoke with recently shared that she worked with a client who was CFO of a large, thriving organization. The results of the initial verbal 360 interviews conducted by the coach indicated that the CFO's direct reports didn't trust him because they didn't know him.   He didn't really open up about anything personally at work.   He stayed focused on the job, the work at hand, and upcoming deadlines.   The CFO didn't see it as his place to open up about his philosophy of leadership or his values.

As a result, his direct reports didn't know anything about him and didn't have a high level of trust with this new leader.   The CFO failed to engage in small talk with direct reports or ask them about themselves, their career goals, or what was important to them.   Some of the comments from his 360 indicated that he would come to them and ask, "Where are you

224

with that update?" or "So, here's the deal... I need you to get this done by Friday." He was very transactional in his interactions with people.

His coach used the holistic philosophy and coached him as a whole person, rather than only the business person. To be an effective leader and inspire others to follow him and accomplish more, he was supported in figuring out how to open up in an authentic way, show that he cared, and that he was supportive of his staff and others. He was called on to be open, accessible, and show himself, the whole person.

His coach used this strategy: Start small and experiment. She shares, "It is not like at his next team meeting he is supposed to go and bare his soul. Instead, he is invited ask himself, 'What are some things I want to strategically start doing to share with people that serve better leadership?' It is more than being open for openness sake. It is about what will serve the greater leadership."

> *"Start small and experiment."*

In another coaching scenario, a coach used the strategy of helping a client grow in self-awareness in order to make decisions from a core sense of being. The coach shared that she was working with a strong, focused business leader in a situation where his business was going through tremendous

225

growth.   This leader was being really stretched because he was in the biggest, most significant role he had ever been in. Through the coaching process, he recognized that he was telegraphing his stress and panic to his team.   He wanted to figure out how to be centered and how to keep the team inspired as they experienced a roller coaster of change.

He and his coach explored various ways to manage this situation. The coach asked, "What will feel inspiring to people?   What can you do to help people feel inspired and to help people follow you through this?"   They generated a short list of things for the group and that were meaningful to him so that he could convey his vision in an inspiring manner.   He realized that leading people is more than meeting the numbers.   His leadership of the team and his leadership vision fulfilled one of his lifelong dreams about growing an organization.

To achieve this vision, he shared with his coach what he thought it meant for their customers and what the team could do to solve their customers' biggest challenges.   His coach encouraged him to put his vision and daily conversations with staff in language that included feeling language and inspirational language that had meaning and purpose behind it.   As he took this first step, he experienced how valuable it was for people to hear his vision as a leader and to hear from them how they felt about it and could contribute to it.   By his ability to stay out of his comfort zone, to express openness in service of helping the team through their transition, he helped the team to stay on purpose, inspired, and feel connected to each other and the greater good.

In another coaching scenario shared by a different executive coach, the corporate leader worked for a company experiencing exponential growth. The client was very goal-driven and intense, with very clearly defined goals and objectives. Through coaching, he became aware of the level of intensity he put into planning and visualizing his end result. Part of his intensity was a creative force or energy. The other part was a nervous force, driven by his fear of failure and apprehension of success. He was literally exhausting himself because he was working so hard to achieve success while trying equally hard to diminish his fear and insecurity.

As a strategy, his coach asked him what it will take for him to create space in the day to stop and breathe every so often so he became aware of his own internal drive. By becoming more mindful, he was preparing to develop sensitivity and understanding about his creative drive and balance both forces more effectively. The client explored with his coach what behaviors he engaged in when he felt fearful or nervous. He discovered that when he became aware that fear was driving him, he had the ability to pause and name the fear. His coach helped him to see that because we overcompensate when fear is

227

involved, to name the fear instead of being driven by the fear is to be powerful through vulnerability.

He chose to test a new strategy at work. He paused in the course of the day and recognized the energy that was driving him in that moment. He then was able to breathe into it, name what the fear was, and then make a choice. He could make the choice to continue feeling the fear, or do something different. The coach explained, "If someone doesn't name the fear, the fear is controlling them, like a marionette. We are like a puppet being pulled on the strings of fear." The coach asked the client to choose when he wanted to be a puppeteer.

The client used the strategy and found that when he named the fear, it was like putting his hands on the strings of the puppet; he had control over his feelings and a greater self-awareness. When he named the fear, he was accessing his own vulnerability. He became aware that when he got fearful, he responded by being overactive and super intense. His coach helped him see that this was a covering up, defensive behavior. The leader learned to pause, breathe, label the fear, and then make a choice. The result was powerful and accessible leadership of his team. He learned that what was driving him was draining him, and to be more effective actually meant to do less; in this case, to use purposeful activity. As he did this, he experienced increased success in his leadership role.

Vulnerability involves being self-aware, being honest, and being courageous. The first step for clients is learning to be compassionate with one's self. Growing in self-awareness empowers a person to be honest with who they are, the way they show up in situations, and with others.

> *"Vulnerability involves being self-aware, being honest, and being courageous."*

Coaches are called upon to be very aware of what is going on with clients internally, and to encourage them to be honest with themselves, to be courageous, then to make a choice. Clients who are compassionate with themselves and supported along the way by their coaches become aware and grow and achieve results more effectively.

One coach I spoke with worked with a client who had very low self- awareness regarding the way he was perceived by others and of the negative impact his behaviors and words often had on those around him. After coaching this client to develop vulnerability with specific people, his coach laughed and told me, "I eventually came to understand that he couldn't open up to risk being vulnerable but he could be charming." The coach asked the client about testing a new behavior for two weeks to experience the outcomes. This dominant leader, who ignored others and stayed continuously on his cell phone making

229

business deals, was challenged to do two things: 1) hang up on cell phone calls when he got out of his car to walk into the office building and 2) when entering his office in the morning to greet people, make eye contact, smile, and say some pleasantry. This simple change resulted in increased positive interactions with others as well as positive comments from virtually everyone on his post 360 review. The lesson from this coaching scenario is that little steps to connect are effective.

> *"The lesson from this coaching scenario is that little steps to connect are effective."*

CONCERNS AND CAUTIONS

Coaches use care when clients step outside their comfort zones to risk vulnerability. Key things to remember are:

1) Create safety first so that clients feel safe enough to venture outside their comfort zone.

2) Start from where the client is now. Explore what they are capable of at this very moment in time.

3) Talk about the system they are operating in and whether or not it is safe and/or appropriate to appear vulnerable.

4) Explore what type of support system they have in place.

5) Ask about flexibility so that clients know where and when to apply vulnerability.

One coach I know cautioned that it is very important to go slowly and to work with where the client is now. This coach remembers coaching a body builder in the past. This man was very muscular and intimidating, with an imposing physique. Coaching him took time and the coach felt that they were limited in making progress because the client lacked interest. During one session, the coach talked about discontinuing. This client, a very senior level leader, responded by breaking down and sobbing. He shared that he had grown up in an abusive home and had built up a tough outer shell as a defense.

The coach used this story as a reminder that when someone is pushed to open up, coaches must be skilled, careful, and proceed slowly. The tougher the shell, the more vulnerable the client may be inside. It takes finesse for coaches to deal with these open wounds. Once a client is open and feels open to injury, coaches proceed carefully and with compassion.

POSSIBLE OUTCOMES WHEN LEADERS RISK VULNERABILITY

One coach shared a story of a Top 10 business leader she had worked with in a global organization. This leader ran the product engineering segment of the business. Senior leadership thought he could be a next top leader so they put him in charge of running the largest division, which included sales

231

and marketing. This was a huge risk for this leader and for the company. He was someone who, by nature, was somewhat different in his view of leadership. He leaned into the difference. There was a huge amount of skepticism about him being successful since he was unfamiliar with sales and marketing. He was someone who really knew how to connect with people and he talked about his own humbling experience coming into the sales team; he came with humility. He won over the sales team. Instead of being the expert, he was deeply connected with who he was as a person, which helped him to be humble and vulnerable as a leader in this new situation.

Through his work with his coach, he became very clear about his own character, his own values, and his own belief in the company. As a result, he was able to hold himself as a learner and partner to the whole organization. People were surprised by this because his approach was outside the norm for senior leaders in this organization. He came in and said, "I don't know what you know. We can learn from each other." As a result, the business became incredibly successful because he took a servant leadership approach. He went on sales calls; he sat and listened to direct reports and colleagues. He was great with the customers. He was willing to be fully centered and very open. This coach remarked that this leader is still one of the best examples of someone being willing to risk being vulnerable and being a great leader.

Executive coach Eric Kaufmann, for the purposes of self-development and growth, chose to spend one year alone in a remote cabin, alone with his thoughts. He shared that it was one of the most agonizing experiences and also one resulting in profound states of accelerated learning, self-discovery, and growth. We each have relationships with others and we also have relationships with our selves. After months of being alone in the wilderness, he became so immersed in self-loathing and self-hate that he felt he was legitimately suicidal for a period of time. He was vulnerable to his own darkness; to his own demons. It wasn't being vulnerable to the elements of nature or others, it was to the self. Those inner voices rose up after years of silencing, and in the absence of fast-paced work, activity, and social interaction, they became a roar and were overwhelming.

> *"We each have relationships with others and we also have relationships with our selves."*

How was he different as a result? Eric shares, "I am far more forgiving to myself for having navigated through that particular challenge. The gift of vulnerability for me was perspective. Having faced those things that I never wanted to face, being open to injury, being open to those experiences I closed off for so many years, was difficult. In the stillness those inner voices came through with such intensity; yet I didn't kill myself and didn't die". Instead, he learned to accept them just as a part of the total inner experience. He marveled, "That inner self-loathing subsided by 85% after that experience. It was huge. It was life changing. I, to this day, do not engage in a lot of self-critical self-beating because those voices that were responsible for the self-beating have diminished significantly. We have changed our relationship."

CONCLUSION

Leaders have the opportunity to build a culture of trust and deep loyalty by showing vulnerability in certain circumstances. Vulnerability-invited trust helps people to realize they often share the same fears, goals, and challenges as their peers. Showing vulnerability is the one thing that empowers a leader to perform at their highest level, both transforming their organizations and also themselves.

Coaches can help their clients explore circumstances and when they want to show vulnerability by asking good questions and holding the space for clients to do self-exploration.
Questions like these help clients view each situation through the lens of vulnerability:

- What will it look like if you appear vulnerable?
- What will you say?

- How will you behave?
- How will you feel?
- How do you think people will react?
- What end result do you think you will achieve?

Helping clients reconnect to their higher vision of leadership and their organization's success helps them to connect the risk they are taking with the end result they want to achieve.

- What is the highest vision you hold for yourself as a leader? For the organization? For your team?
- What positive result will happen if you are vulnerable?
- How will your sharing your vulnerability help others?
- What will it convey?
- How will you be remembered?
- If you decide not to share your vulnerability in this situation, how will you feel about it later?

Asking such questions often helps clients access and examine their fears, those voices that whisper at night and stand in the way of success. Clients often realize during this process that facing fears of being vulnerable means laying themselves open to injury, facing fears of being exposed, being criticized, or being rejected. In the very moment of being vulnerable with a clear and strong purpose of higher intent comes the triumph.

"In the very moment of being vulnerable with a clear and strong purpose of higher intent comes the triumph."

Marie Snidow, CMC, SPHR has over 23 years of combined experience in talent management, leadership development, talent development, and executive coaching. She utilizes her knowledge of leadership and high potential development to assist her clients in growing their leadership capabilities and removing barriers to success along the way.

Marie is AVP of Leadership Development for a global company specializing in benefits, insurance, and wealth management services. She designs and implements leadership development programs, high potential programs, and mentoring programs to grow top talent. Marie also manages the executive coaching of all leadership levels.

Marie holds a Master's degree in Counseling, is a certified Senior Professional in Human Resources (SPHR ®) and a Certified Master Coach. She is also certified to use many leadership assessments, such as Hogan Assessments, Emotional Intelligence Leadership EQi2.0, and Center for Creative Leadership Benchmarks 360.

As a leader in her community, Marie has most recently served as an Advisory Board Member for Seton Hospital Northwest in Austin and was a recent speaker regarding leadership at the Austin Women in Technology Forum.

COACHING: THE ART OF MANAGEMENT

Brian McReynolds

Coaching is more than a profession or industry; it is an opportunity to change the culture. Using coaching skills personally, in business, and as a leader will enhance your outcomes and engage the people around you. With the growth of coaching comes new opportunities to increase the impact of managers in the workplace.

> *"Coaching is more than a profession or industry; it is an opportunity to change the culture."*

THE CASE FOR MANAGERS

Management as a business term has gone out of style. It has been replaced by the trendy and also elusive word leadership. Management is being used interchangeably with the dirtiest of business terms, micromanagement. The micromanager is inclined to exert control over others by monitoring and accessing business processes step by step with the tendency to refrain from the delegation of decision making. Simply put, the micromanager tells their employees what to do and how to do it. The resulting series of unfortunate actions ensures that the accountability for failure is the only task that is truly delegated.

In many of my management workshops, I devote time to defining several terms to clarify our use of language and relationships. These terms include: Mentorship, Coaching, Counseling, Codependent Relationship, and Management. Defining these relationships sets the stage for understanding the role of a coaching style of management. The unspoken truths we will uncover are that an effective manager focuses on processes and coaches people. The work is less about work and more about relationships and growth. Think about it: it is fairly easy to find someone who can do the tasks that define work. It is more challenging to find someone who gets along with others, effectively manages energy levels, is open and accepting, assumes responsibility for their actions, and who supports the goals of the organization.

> *"Defining these relationships sets the stage for understanding the role of a coaching style of management."*

I personally decided to become a certified coach because at some point during my twenty-plus-year career in management, I realized that 90% of my time was dedicated to helping my employees evolve and gain greater awareness through identifying challenges and opportunities then developing solutions. Even though any one of these employees could easily carry out the tasks involved in work, every one of them struggled with resolving personality differences, practicing effective communication, and establishing healthy boundaries.

Recently I was a keynote speaker for a company's annual meeting. Prior to the event, I met with the Vice President of the company to discuss key topics that would be addressed. The gentleman was extremely concerned that we focus primarily on leadership and not management. Leadership, it seems, was the new term for savvy business. "Our company," he said, "wants to grow young leaders, not managers."

I thought a lot about what he said and ended up including management while explaining the differences between management and leadership, and what we really benefit from learning. Management, you see, is becoming a lost art. The process of honing good management skills is being left by the wayside to embrace leadership hyperbole and big ideas. Unfortunately, the effect of focusing on the development of leadership alone and overlooking the development of a solid management force is the creation of a conflict-driven workforce run by unskilled, empowered micromanagers. Leadership is absolutely important, and it is built with solid front line managers. Solid managers are the people who streamline processes, empower their workforce, manage conflict-driven grievances, and provide a solid foundation for leaders to build upon. In short, solid management skills involve coaching and create balanced management of an organization; balanced managers use assertiveness blended with fairness and the ability to create cohesion along with coaching techniques.

240

Underdeveloped managers, on the other hand, tend to utilize management skills that are unsustainable such as believing they can actually manage people. So, as a better alternative, resurrect the art of skilled management by looking to certain coaching concepts such as the power of questioning and growing awareness which help to provide a sustainable, growth-based business.

> *"...resurrect the art of skilled management by looking to certain coaching concepts..."*

TELLING VERSUS ASKING

The intricacies of boundaries and communication are often undeveloped skills. Managers without these skills become dependent on the control that they exert over others for their success. The expectation of perfection and success leads them into a pattern of telling their employees what to do, thus creating co-dependency. More effective is asking them for their solution or an approach to something; this creates competent decision makers.

The unsustainable pattern tends to be caused by fear of failure, lack of solid communication skills, undefined boundaries, and the inability to effectively engage employees in the organization's success. The bottom line is that the training for

241

these managers is inadequate. There is, instead, an untenable expectation that our managers can perform the work better or more effectively than their employee; this leads the manager toward dictating with specific work directives. In other words, it sets up an atmosphere of employees being told what to do and how to do it. This process is both time consuming and it also requires a tremendous amount of energy. This antiquated process, although it may have merit under some circumstances, actually causes organizational underdevelopment. A better belief is to empower employee growth by asking, among other things, what the next step is, or how to prevent the issue in the first place. This empowers an employee to become responsible for the outcome of a job-related concern as well as for their personal success. The art of mastering management is creating a new organizational structure where the employees are the leading experts in their fields and the manager ensures that that the process, instead of the person, is well-managed. This means train managers in the coaching competencies to truly develop them as effective managers.

Ironically, unsustainable organizational structures may be the source of some of these job related challenges. The traditional hierarchical chart promotes a top down control structure that leaves the foundation (the common employee) undeveloped. The organization itself can unwittingly transfer a message of required perfection to the manager that causes a developmental freeze for the organization as a whole. This message can be conveyed by a lack of organizational support for personal growth or professional training opportunities, and / or an expectation of strict adherence to increasingly stringent performance standards. In addition, the organization may require the manager to provide a level of stability that seems to maintain the status quo. The status quo, although providing a temporary sense of false security, becomes stagnant at some point and prevents positive organizational evolution. Managers serve more of a vital role by doing their own job well while fostering the growth and development of the employees and thus the allowing for constructive, indispensable change. For this reason coaching employees supports organizational health.

Control practices are kept because of the human desire for stability; most humans are designed to be uncomfortable with change. Luckily, there are a few leaders who instinctively know that organizational change can be cutting edge and know that new vision is healthy and productive. To that end organizational development can be enhanced by resurrecting the art of management with coaching because leaders build on the savvy efforts of trained managers. The organization can foster growth by inserting a new organizational model where the control flows from the inside out instead of the top down. Each employee is part of ensuring the success of the whole.

"Each employee is part of ensuring the success of the whole."

QUESTIONING AND GROWING AWARENESS

Coaching provides a platform to help my clients understand both the intricacies and simplicities of solid management practices. This platform is based on two important skills: communication and healthy boundaries.

Often times, employees are promoted into managerial positions based on the fact that they are good employees with strong work ethics. They are placed in these management positions with little to no training on how to actually be a balanced manager. The simple and obvious solution is to include coach training as a step in the promotion process. This ensures that the new manager has the ability to be effective in interpersonal relationships, effective communication skills, and knowledge to engage then motivate employees while supporting a focus on long-term outcomes.

This type of management calls for coaching skill development in all managers with responsibility for decisions and outcomes. Opportunities for growth and learning are given by empowering individuals in the organization to take responsibility for their actions, even if that means being allowed to fail. So, if the goal is to create a vital organization, then start with understanding a healthier management practice: A Coaching Style of Management.

COACHING STYLE OF MANAGEMENT

Coaching Style of Management practices are simple to learn and use. They become a sustainable and successful part of creating a vital organization. Coaching Style of Management practices are based on two skills: healthy boundary setting and communication, plus five strategies: clarify the statement, seek input, gain consensus, set expectations, and follow through.

> *"Coaching Style of Management practices are based on two skills: healthy boundary setting and communication, plus five strategies: clarify the statement, seek input, gain consensus, set expectations, and follow through."*

First, it is imperative to have a clear understanding of healthy boundaries. A boundary is a limit that protects the integrity of your day, your energy, and your spirit. It protects the health of your relationships and the sovereignty of your heart. Time is an example of a major boundary. Meetings, a major source of boundary encroachment, can be set with intentional safeguards. I typically like to keep my meetings scheduled for under an hour, a deliberately short period of time to accomplish work, out of respect for the time requirements of my attendees. Inevitably there will be employees show up late or who divert concentration from the business at hand. The cause for lateness is generally one crisis or another and the diversions can

245

be funny and enjoyable, both impact the schedule. The various reasons individuals may encroach on the meeting time are beside the point. The particular boundary is the point: in this example time is a boundary and the scheduled meeting is the line drawn to guard its integrity. If someone cannot respect a set meeting time, then they have squandered a resource for you and the others that attend the meeting. Instead of discussing the employees' reasons for being late or diverting focus, which might create defensive attention toward personal failings, managers can learn to discuss the occurrences in terms of a boundary. Boundaries create a neutral talking point that doesn't suggest a personal attack. The neutrality allows both employer and employee to discuss expectations and establish a healthy process for improvement. Healthy boundary setting is the first required coaching style of management skill.

Second, clear communication is essential for success. Through utilization of different types of cues and techniques from nonverbal to written and verbal communication, a good manager can avoid miscommunication in most circumstances. Nonverbal communication techniques include tone, gestures, facial expressions, and tempo. Some important tips are to maintain eye contact and mirror the other person's body language. This helps to put the other person at ease and to build rapport. Verbal communication includes use of positive language and ensuring that your employees clearly understand

246

your expectations. In addition, the manager is well served to clearly hear the employees' concerns as an essential part of true communication. Clear communication is the second required coaching style of management skill.

In order to build healthy boundaries and communicative relationships in the workplace, a manager must develop an overall toolbox of skills and strategies. This toolbox will help to manage the unique relationship that exists as soon as an employee becomes a manager with the team of employees now reporting to him or her for guidance. The manager must consciously set aside time to develop the skills and strategies in their toolbox and realize that a combination of methodologies will create success; success is built with time and experience. Developing these management skills and strategies will empower the manager to have specific advantages: the understanding of how to gather and use productive information through developing skills of communication and boundary setting, and the facilitation of working with teams that provide group cohesion. The five strategies specifically support the belief system that the work is to manage a process instead of people.

"In order to build healthy boundaries and communicative relationships in the workplace, a manager must develop an overall toolbox of skills and strategies."

The first of these five strategies is to clarify the statement.

"...clarify the statement."

Managers can find themselves stuck between a sense of personal failure and the desire to move forward in the process. Through this strategy's technique, the manager is going to create distance among themselves, the employee, and the situation. Ultimately, they will try to envision themselves looking into the situation from outside of a window. By creating this imaginary distance, the manager is then able to gain perspective over the problem. It is most important to be impartial and non-judgmental. The specific intent of this step is to remove any finger pointing toward the individual. This means beginning to view the role from a coaching perspective instead of attempting to manage an individual or team. Thus the manager learns how to choose language based on intent and to separate the situation from the person. In this manner, the manager is then able to make a non-judgmental assessment. While the concept of managing an individual or team begins to change during this process, you still want to verify your statement with the individual or the team. You may very well already know the answer; this technique helps to build rapport and eliminate any misunderstandings. This both helps the individual feel as though the manager has truly listened to their concerns and they have begun to believe that they are supported. Through this initial communication step, a healthy boundary has been set with a clarification of the statement that will assist a manager who begins working through the issue.

The next of the five strategies is to seek input. In this step the manager purposefully begins to view the situation as working toward the desired goal. The goal is to promote ownership of the solution with the individual or team because people seek the opportunity to grow, and even make mistakes, in order to become functioning members of a team. If a manager forces lessons on the team they will stunt their growth and be forced into making all of the decisions them self. It is therefore important to ask for the individual or team input on the resolution. Ask the employees what it is specifically that they want to achieve. Powerful questions empower the manager to guide employees in establishing feasible goals. In my experience people have been truly more receptive to moving toward a positive goal instead of away from a negative outcome.

Another key portion of this strategy is to practice active listening skills and often to also refrain from responding or filling in the blanks. Let the individual or the team answer the questions and clarify their own statements. The manager is simply there to guide the process in a positive manner by asking powerful questions and restating what they thought they heard. This moves the responsibility from the manager to the individual.

The next management strategy is to gain consensus. One can think of this as the decision making portion of the management strategies. While there are several types of decision making styles the goal of this step is to empower a participative outcome. The difficulty of participative decision making is that it ultimately requires excellent communication skills on the part of the manager. The advantages to the participative decision are that the individual or team members feel listened to and have a sense a commitment to the decision. Thus the final decision carries a clear statement of responsibility. As the manager is honing communication skills there are advantages and disadvantages to using other types of decision making styles; the participative decision is the healthiest choice in the end. Unilateral decisions, for example, are effective in crisis situations, for use with uncomplicated decisions, and also for extremely young teams. The expert style of decision making is useful when trying to manage liability or when one person has advanced expertise in the matter. Both of these decision types can be useful; neither one allows for the development of the team or individual.

> *"The advantages to the participative decision are that the individual or team members feel listened to and have a sense a commitment to the decision."*

The fourth strategy is to set expectations. While it may be obvious, I find that many managers skip this step. It is extremely important in every circumstance expectations are set because it defines the role as a manager and lays out a path for individual or team success. The goal of the strategy here is to communicate what will be the expected outcome for the situation. It will set specific dates, times, and goals for the individual or team. I find that setting expectations is much like putting an action plan in place. These types of plans can be formulated through personnel evaluations, operating agreements, key performance indicators, and even personal improvement plans. These plans become living documents, demonstrating quantitative measures to document progress and expectations.

Setting expectations has an element of manager oversight that allows for evaluating whether the responses are actionable, can be accomplished within the time frame, and are pertinent. Once the manager has defined the situation and actively listened and sought input, a determination must then be made as to what part of the input received falls within the proper boundaries for the situation. There is some leeway here as the manager can purposely allow the team to face failure as a way to grow their experiences. In most cases the manager remains responsible to guide the team toward a reasonable chance for success.

The final management strategy is follow-through. This is based on having gained consensus. The manager is dealing with the actual outcome and how it compares to the expected outcome. In this regard the manager is like an accountability coach. The manager will want to evaluate how the goals, dates, and times that were established while setting expectations were achieved.   It is imperative to take action as a follow up.

> **"It is imperative to take action as a follow up."**

There are three measures of follow through depending on the desired result: reprimand, reward, and recognize.   All three measures are linked to the manager's evaluation process with the ultimate goal being justification of merit raises for appropriate performance or, on the other hand, justification for a reprimand for poor performance.   If it is determined that the expectations were either missed or ignored, the manager will reprimand the employee in some way for violating that boundary.   This can be achieved in several ways depending on the number of violations and history of the employee.   Refer to the company's written policy for action; it is important to do only what is appropriate and also effective to achieve the desired result.   Documenting the individual or team failure to meet expectations is critical. Many times a simple coaching session is a great beginning to this process.   Conversations with an individual remain private, while conversations regarding the team remain within the team. If the follow through involves coaching an employee, the manager will want to use all five strategies again to re-clarify, seek input, gain consensus, re-set expectations, and follow through on the new outcome.   Remember that it is important for the employees to be a part of the process, and it is important for the manager to follow through after the expectations have been met or missed.   Taking action will build team trust.

For the individuals or teams that meet the expectations, the manager will want to determine whether and what reward or recognition is appropriate. This decision involves a judgment call on behalf of the manager in addition to getting input. It is important to document achievements for those who meet or exceed expectations as well. Many employees are completely content in most cases being recognized for their efforts and gain satisfaction by being involved in the process. For extraordinary measures achieved, offer a reward. Rewards can consist of a free lunch, a half day off, recommendation for a departmental reward, a company picnic, or even a team t-shirt. Really it is whatever suits the accomplishment. Rewards can also be turned into incentive programs that are budgeted for on an annual basis.

"For extraordinary measures achieved, offer a reward."

The three R's make a difference because employees want poor performance to be challenged and appreciate being acknowledged for good performance. Unfortunately some organizations shy away from the three R's because of the misperception of their constituents that the workforce is wasting time or taxpayer money. This misperception, too, is a boundary; conveying the importance of recognition for both a job well done and a job poorly done is the responsibility of a manager using a coaching style.

THE MANAGER WITH A COACHING STYLE

Questioning employees about how they might solve a problem or even how they perceive the issue instead of telling employees the answer or perception begins to make management synonymous with a coaching style. This balance provides fertile ground to empower leadership to flourish. Keep in mind that each situation provides an opportunity for a process to be managed instead of individuals to be controlled. Each situation provides an opportunity for an individual to grow, gain awareness of healthy behaviors and processes, and to feel heard.

A manager with a coaching style is a blend between a team builder and a general. This manager is effectively assertive while creating a synergistic environment to bring people together within the whole. A coaching style of management means effectively managing processes and understanding that, by doing so, the manager provides the opportunity for individual growth. Often there are situations where an individual struggles within the boundaries that a manager has set. Even if the individual has good reason for the struggle, they may be unable to find a way to meet the goal. By setting boundaries surrounding the process the manager is then able to put the success of the individual with the individual. If the manager were to make concessions for an individual, they sacrifice the trust of the whole and relinquish their boundaries as well.

254

Prior to learning this technique, I had an employee with a substance abuse issue. Nonetheless, this person had been a great employee in the past, was well liked, showed concerned for others, and was willing to help; they only fully functioned some of the time. I felt bad for the employee. I felt bad for the employee's family. At some level I must have actually felt responsible for helping the individual to remain employed because I continued to provide opportunities for training and growth even when the employee came to work smelling of alcohol. Finally, the employee was caught in a compromised condition while driving a work vehicle. Even with this final straw, I made sure that multiple chances for change were given by assisting with enrollment in substance abuse programs and counseling. In the end, the employee was unable to overcome the issue. I have since reflected that the hard times the employee faced preceding termination were an opportunity to choose something different. Each time I made an excuse for the employee I put my organization at risk and disregarded their disregard for the policies and boundaries. I have since discovered that the success of an individual lies with that particular individual. I can only provide the environment and the resources that enrich their success. Fertile ground can grow an entire garden from just a tiny seed.

> *"...provide the environment and the resources that enrich their success. Fertile ground can grow an entire garden from just a tiny seed."*

CONCLUSION

The concept of the Coaching Style of Management makes it possible to link the term management with leadership. This is accomplished primarily through the resourcefulness of questioning and empowering awareness to grow, thus empowering leadership to grow within the organization. Having developed a strong, well-managed foundation, leadership naturally follows suit. For many years, I spent time developing my employees by providing training and allowing them to be responsible for developing and maintaining their programs. Today, my organization basically runs itself. I continue being amazed with how far my employees have come. They sign themselves up for training sessions and work groups, they develop public education days, and ensure that we are adhering to all laws and regulations. As they have been given more responsibility, their creativity and willingness have also grown. While I provide formal rewards, my employees' greatest reward truly is the work that they do well. Conversely, my greatest reward has been assisting in the growth of these individuals. If the truth be told, this success has been accomplished through the dismantling of a traditional, hierarchal organization and engaging in the coaching style of management.

> *"... this success has been accomplished through the dismantling of a traditional, hierarchal organization and engaging in the coaching style of management."*

Brian McReynolds is a Certified Professional Coach and received his B.S. in Civil Engineering from Virginia Military Institute. He is a professional engineer with over 20 years of experience in the municipal public works industry. He was recognized for his contributions by being named a Public Works Leadership Fellow, which means he will mentor up-and-coming public works professionals.

He currently manages and leads a staff of over 100 people for the City of Waynesboro, Virginia, Department of Public Works. He is responsible for a total department budget of $15 million, and is often in charge of multi-million dollar projects such as treatment plant expansion, bridge repairs, storm water infrastructure mitigation, or landfill closure to name a few.

In addition to his work with city government, Brian is an adjunct Professor with Blue Ridge Community College where he teaches Management and Leadership classes. Brian is also a facilitator for the Chamber of Commerce's Leadership Greater Augusta which strengthens participants for personal, organizational, and community leadership. He currently resides in Staunton, Virginia with his two children, Gabrielle and Ty, and enjoys making custom designed rustic furniture.

Brian@InstituteforAppliedLeadership.org

COACHING FOR MASTER LEARNERS IN ACADEMIA

Julie Binter

Imagine a workplace where learning and innovation are the norm. Where challenges are welcomed and resolved successfully. Where people rebound quickly from adversity and change while focusing on the positive side of the experience. Where people treat each other respectfully and fairly, even when experiencing conflict.

To some this may sound like a very idealistic and hard to achieve culture that requires years of effort. In many workplaces, this type of environment is considered unrealistic. At the same time leaders and independent contributors frequently turn to internal and external trainers, consultants, and coaches to build programs and facilitate interventions that will move people toward this ideal. On a very basic level we know it can be difficult to achieve and we want it anyway. The desire for a healthy and high performing workplace culture is incredibly strong.

This ideal workplace is possible with an investment of time, effort and the development of master learners. What is a master learner? How does coaching support the development of master learners? What can leaders and organizations learn from the academic world to create their own ideal workplace?

259

The answers to these questions are the focus of this chapter.

DEFINING A MASTER LEARNER

A master learner is an individual of any age who is self-aware, has an insatiable curiosity, plus perseveres and remains resilient in the face of challenges. This definition begins with the elements of emotional intelligence and then expands beyond that. Master learners take responsibility for their own learning and are on a quest for continuous improvement and growth. Being a master learner is about using internal qualities and translating them into external actions that can increase an individual's professional success in any environment. In the workplace, master learners positively impact engagement, innovation, and retention, all of which contribute to organizational success.

> *"A master learner is an individual of any age who is self-aware, has an insatiable curiosity, plus perseveres and remains resilient in the face of challenges."*

Trial and error is an essential component when developing master learners. Finding the right formula for each individual and organization can be time consuming or it can be more efficient when planned with intention. The academic world can serve as a great resource because developing master learners happens to be their business. Because I work in academia, the

260

examples come from this world. These examples are applicable in all industries and work places.

> *"Finding the right formula for each individual and organization ... more efficient when planned with intention."*

ACADEMIA AS A RESOURCE FOR ORGANIZATIONS

The primary goal of higher education is building the capacity of students to be successful in the dynamic and ever-changing workplaces of today. Universities and colleges are unique because they can offer challenging academic programs and impactful on-campus employment experiences. When approached intentionally and strategically, academia can ensure its students have an increased capacity for success in the work world when they graduate. In doing this, academia is striving to develop master learners.

The academic world is an ideal place to develop master learners due to its existing focus on learning, growth and development. What we have learned over time is that those individuals responsible for creating the environment to support master learners are more successful when they are master learners themselves. Leaders and individuals in positions at all levels, faculty, staff, and administrators, may or may not have the qualities and experience to do this important work.

261

Many universities invest a large portion of their resources to support and develop faculty as they have the most face-time with students in the classroom. This approach makes sense and also reduces the time and attention given to staff and administrators who support students outside the classroom through essential services and on-campus employment opportunities. Staff training and development departments in academia are responsible for supporting these employees. These departments are very focused, selective, and creative to deliver impactful learning opportunities on a modest budget.

At my university, our employee development department facilitates leadership programs and skills workshops with the master learner in mind. By providing the foundation for staff to become master learners, we are supporting the organization's goal to develop our students. Through a lot of trial and error, we have discovered that one of the best and most cost-effective ways to do this is through improving and enhancing the coaching skills of our leaders and managers.

HOW COACHING HELPS

Coaching, as defined by the International Coaching Federation, models the traits of a master learner: self-awareness, curiosity, and resilience; it also develops the skills of master learners.

Coaches partner with clients to:

- Discover, clarify, and align self-directed goals.
- Increase self-discovery and unlock potential.
- Identify their own solutions and strategies.
- Take ownership and responsibility for action.
- Improve their overall outlook and leadership skills.

Coaches use:

- Discovery-based assessments, inventories, a solution-focus, and frameworks to increase awareness.
- Powerful questioning and active listening.
- Client-generated actions, accountability, and proactive ways of managing challenges that increase perseverance and resilience.

Considering the limited amount of resources available for the development of staff, an ideal starting place to introduce basic coaching skills is an existing leadership development program. An alternative may be a mentor program. The internal training and development team can utilize a coaching approach during consultations and work with subject matter experts. If internal or external trainers have the ICF-approved training in coaching as called for in the Association for Talent Development (ATD) core competency model, then they are equipped to offer training based on the ICF competencies for others to be coaches within the organization.

As coaching skills are improved within leaders and mentors, and a coaching approach is incorporated across an organization; the foundation for a coaching culture is laid. A coaching culture will increase the qualities of master learners in staff who can then turn around and support the development of master learner traits in student employees.

> *"As coaching skills are improved within leaders and mentors, and a coaching approach is incorporated across an organization; the foundation for a coaching culture is laid."*

COACHING AS A TRAINER IN ACADEMIA

In the fall of 2012, I accepted a position within the training and development department of a large university. One of my primary responsibilities was facilitating a multi-day supervisor development program.

When I arrived, the program format consisted of five full days spread out over a three-week period. Participants had a diverse mix of skills as supervisors, with experience ranging anywhere from one day to twenty years. Subject matter experts from the human resources department delivered most of the content in a lecture format with very little time for inquiry, practice, and action steps for implementation. This training model was the complete opposite of a coaching approach and failed to improve the self-awareness, curiosity, and perseverance of the learners.

As I reviewed past evaluation results, I noticed that participants had a strong desire to learn and practice performance management skills during the course. Additionally, participants specifically expressed interest in improving their coaching skills to help increase accountability in their employees. They knew they wanted to increase their coaching skills and they wanted to know how to do it.

As a long-time learning professional and recently certified coach, I immediately set out to fulfill this request and began researching and testing different options over the next two years.

The initial priorities:
- Choose a simple and effective model for use by any supervisor at any level on any type of challenge.
- Practice skills using real-life supervisor challenges.

During the first year, participants experimented with several step-by-step coaching models. They found them too complex, unnatural, and tedious. I spent more time explaining the models and participants spent less time practicing.

A desire for a better approach was solidified when these same participants returned several months later and could not

265

remember any of the coaching models or the basic concepts of asking open-ended questions.

In rethinking my initial priorities, I realized that a focus on developing coaching skills meant the supervisors were prepared to access the tools at any time, informally and formally.

The focus shifted to:
- Listening skills
- Asking open-ended questions
- Recognizing the difference between coaching and telling

Instead of adding additional content to an already full program agenda, I kept things simple with a less is more approach that proved to be successful. Participants were able to zero in and practice basic coaching skills, such as reflective listening, asking relevant open-ended questions, and allowing for more silence so their partner could answer for themselves. Several participants commented on how positive they felt during the exercises in both roles. The ability to experience and see the power of coaching was very impactful. They left the training with enough confidence to apply their coaching skills and returned with powerful stories about the unexpected positive changes they started seeing in the performance of their staff.

"...less is more..."

One such example was a manager in the leadership program. He shared that his student employees frequently asked questions that he had already answered. He provided answers repeatedly to save time and was unsure how to redirect his staff. He also wondered why his staff remained quiet during one-on-one meetings. In his mind, the goal of these meetings was to proactively address challenges before they occurred yet he spent the majority of his day reacting to unexpected things.

After he learned and practiced both his listening and questioning skills in class, he committed to this new approach with his student employees for several weeks. Three weeks later, he called to talk about his progress. He expressed surprise and delight with the results he had achieved in such a short time. Instead of telling the staff the answer, he listened patiently and asked open-ended questions to help the staff identify options and choose the best solution. He also applied this strategy during one-on-one meetings and noticed increased dialogue. He spent time being proactive rather than reactive which in turn created a positive and empowering experience.

Another example is a long-time supervisor who chose to attend the leadership program because she wanted to enhance her ability to develop her staff. She was unsure how to help her direct reports with annual professional development goals. Before the training, her process was to select several options for each person and ask them to choose one for the year. She was frustrated because very few staff accomplished their goal. She frequently asked each person how she could help, and did not receive any feedback.

After learning about and practicing how to ask open-ended questions, she became very excited and shared a big realization with the large group. She was telling her staff what to do instead of asking them to choose their own professional development goal. She planned to change her approach using coaching skills and empower her staff to take ownership of their own development.

She returned later to share what happened. She initially talked to each individual to explain what she had learned in the program about her current approach to setting professional development goals. She then asked each person to take two weeks to identify several goals that they wanted to pursue during the year. She brainstormed several open-ended questions and kept them next to her during the follow-up conversation with each direct report. Her focus for every meeting was to: review the employee's list of options, discuss pros and cons of each, and ask open-ended questions to help that staff person choose action steps and deadlines on one goal. She noticed an immediate change in her staff and shared that several of them had already accomplished their goals in a few months.

The initial success of this training approach for staff was very exciting, and it was just the beginning. Several of the components that contributed to these results were priorities:

- Pre-reading on the goals and benefits of coaching.
- Individual reflection on experiences with coaching.
- Multiple opportunities to discuss and practice coaching skills in small peer groups during the course.
- An option to be coached by a certified coach.
- Post-training practice and reflection.

Experimentation with additional elements supported even greater success:

- Coaching and support from the participant's manager.
- Facilitated opportunities after the training program to refresh and practice coaching skills on a regular basis.

Fortunately, I maintain contact with many of our leadership program participants. After three years, I can confidently say that I am seeing a significant number of our supervisors demonstrating the traits of master learners.

Where I observe this shift most is in coaching sessions with past participants. Their self-awareness of their leadership strengths and weaknesses has expanded. They display an expanded curiosity about the underlying reasons behind staff performance. They respond proactively to the challenges they face.

The most promising outcome of this change is their willingness to model and promote these behaviors with their staff through coaching conversations.

DEVELOP YOUR OWN MASTER LEARNERS

Arriving at the idea to develop employees as master learners within academia was quite easy because we are already engaged in the development of students as master learners. Until I worked in the academic world though, I hadn't considered this option for other types of organizations. After several years of promising outcomes, I truly believe that any leader or organization will greatly benefit from developing master learners in their own workforce. The exciting news is that anyone can capitalize on the lessons learned and shared here to create a customized approach that fits the scenario.

> *"...any leader or organization will greatly benefit from developing master learners in their own workforce."*

If your focus is to develop master learners of individual contributors, start with the three primary traits of a master learner: self-awareness, curiosity, and resilience.

Self-awareness: There are already many options available to trainers and coaches to increase and enhance self-awareness in individuals. Examples include formal and informal self and 360 assessments, individual reflection, and small group activities.

Curiosity: The awareness builders discussed naturally promote curiosity. You can help individuals increase their curiosity even more by encouraging the use of powerful questions for resolving challenges, overcoming obstacles, identifying career goals, and developing innovative solutions.

Resilience: Increasing self-awareness and enhancing a curious mindset will naturally lead to greater resilience and perseverance. To solidify success in this area it is important to encourage individuals to reflect specifically on these three traits.

If your focus is on supervisors or managers to support their teams becoming master learners, introducing and enhancing their basic coaching skills is a great place to start. Have an ICF-trained coach provide training and support to improve their listening skills and ability to access and ask appropriate open-ended questions. Ensure that training is easy to understand and includes multiple opportunities to practice, receive feedback in real time, and reflect on areas for improvement.

"Have an ICF-trained coach provide training and support…"

Supervisors will benefit greatly from continued opportunities to practice and reflect on their coaching skills. Provide an opportunity for supervisors to discuss their progress, ask questions, brainstorm strategies, and continue to practice the basics of coaching with peers. This reinforces the traits of a master learner and strengthens skills.

BEYOND SKILLS: BUILD A CULTURE

If you desire to build an entire organization of master learners, then the goal will be to create a culture that encourages, recognizes, and rewards master learner behaviors. The following options come from my experience in academia.

Evaluate the Existing Culture: At the beginning of this chapter, I asked you to imagine a workplace where learning and innovation are the norm. Where challenges are welcomed and resolved successfully. Where people rebound quickly from adversity and change and focus on the positive side of the experience. Where people treat each other respectfully and fairly, even when experiencing conflict. If this type of environment is appealing, then some questions to consider in this step include:

- How do we support staff development?
- How do we support and encourage innovation?

272

- How do we address challenges?
- How do we respond to change?
- How do we treat each other?

Evaluating the existing culture can be done formally or informally by the training department, the senior leadership team, a human resources representative, or even the manager of a department or team. It will be important to consider the culture from several angles as they all contribute to the ability of staff to be master learners.

Explore the Ideal: You can use the traits of a master learner as a discussion starter to establish which qualities are most important to help the organization achieve its goals:

- Self-awareness – knowledge of one's styles, preferences, strengths, and areas for development
- Insatiable curiosity – continuous search for knowledge
- Resilience – bounce back in the face of challenges
- Responsibility – take ownership appropriately
- Continuous improvement – seek to make things better
- Engagement – enthusiastically show up and contribute
- Innovation – imagine and introduce new things

Use a Coaching Approach: To support the movement toward a coaching culture, use powerful questions to determine the true objective and how you can help. Powerful questions are an essential part of coaching. They start with: what, how, who, where, and when. Powerful questions are open-ended and encourage the other person to generate their own thoughts and ideas. This models the curiosity of a master learner.

> *"Powerful questions are open-ended and encourage the other person to generate their own thoughts and ideas."*

For example, our training department receives many requests for custom consulting projects from leaders across the university aimed at improving staff and team performance. When approached in the past, we asked logistical questions. Now we use open-ended questions during the first conversation to define the existing challenges and desired outcomes before we make a commitment to help. Through powerful questions, we communicate to our stakeholders that they know their situation best and most likely already have the answers. Our role is to help to draw out those answers and co-create an action plan.

Shift Thinking: In the workplace of the past, employees were told what to do and expected to follow directives. Organizations were hierarchical. Decisions were made by senior leaders without any input from staff. In the past several years we have started to see a shift in demographics and mindset. In many workplaces of today managers and leaders are expected to understand motivation, engagement, collaboration, inclusion, and individualized development in order to retain their best talent. Many younger employees enter the workforce expecting to have a voice and want the autonomy to develop their leadership skills and grow their careers. They also crave frequent feedback, mentoring, and coaching. This is a shift from the experience and skill set of longer-term managers and many are seeking alternatives to change their approach.

One way for leaders to be successful during this transition is to shift thinking from accountability to ownership. Accountability thinking limits a manager to believing that he or she has all the answers when employees have questions. Ownership thinking empowers a manager to use a coaching approach that helps an employee to discover their own answers and resolve their own challenges. Additionally, it improves their ability to think analytically and critically about challenges as well as advancing professional development and growth.

Build Credibility: Participating in coaching conversations is a great way to experience and connect to the power of coaching. If there are a limited number of certified coaches available to provide this type of service, consider using a certification program and partner with staff to help them acquire their coaching certification to increase credibility. These individuals will then be prepared to become part of an internal coaching program for leaders.

Promote Success: An often-missed opportunity in building a strong foundation for a culture shift is highlighting success stories. Based on my own experience with coaching, I've seen it lead to increased engagement, improved business results, and focused teams. Collect and share stories of success from across the organization to demonstrate how coaching skills can create master learners. These stories can be shared in the form of a video, a podcast, a feature article in the staff newsletter, in a panel presentation, or during a training session. Promoting the success of others through personal stories will positively impact others' perceptions around the value of coaching.

Measure Results: Demonstrate the power of coaching to leaders with quantitative data. Determine what you want to know before, during, and after any changes you make and create the infrastructure to measure those things. Use the data to show Return on Investment (ROI) and make the case for the continued support of your efforts.

> *"Demonstrate the power of coaching*
> *to leaders with quantitative data."*

CONCLUSION

Master learners are self-aware, highly curious, and resilient in the face of challenges. In the workplace, a master learner's focus on continuous improvement leads to innovative ideas, creative problem-solving and increased organizational success. The academic world has been developing master learners in students for a long time and can serve as a reference for others who want to develop master learners in their own environment.

The employee training department of my academic institution has discovered that improving the coaching skills of supervisors effectively supports the development of master learners, especially when combined with other elements of coaching.

> *"…improving the coaching skills of supervisors effectively supports the development of master learners…"*

Building the skills of master learners takes time, energy, and a deeper-level commitment. If you are striving for a healthy and high performing workplace, developing master learners will result in worthwhile benefits for individuals, leaders, and the organization.

Julie Binter is an organizational development consultant, emotional intelligence trainer, and certified master coach within a large state university in the southwestern United States. She partners with staff, managers, teams, and departments who want to increase their effectiveness both personally and professionally by providing workshops, leadership development programs, assessments, consulting, and coaching.

Julie holds a Bachelor of Arts in Sociology from the University of Minnesota and a Master's in Organizational Development and Leadership from Fielding Graduate University. She is a Certified Master Coach through the Center for Coaching Certification and a Six Seconds EI Master Trainer.

Julie values and promotes continuous improvement and accountability as essential elements of success. She is passionate and committed to delivering engaging and client-centered learning opportunities that inspire people to translate knowledge into action. Her personal mission is to empower others to increase self-awareness, align with their values, and live life with integrity at work, at home, and in the community. As a certified coach, Julie continues to be surprised and delighted by the power of coaching and the amazing outcomes.

juliebinter@yahoo.com

CAREER COACHING: STAYING WITHIN THE LINES
Amy Gamblin

Imagine you are on your career journey and gradually realize that the path you are on is leading you the wrong direction. You stumble along the way because you think that if you stay on that path long enough, perhaps something will change. Maybe a light will shine and all will be revealed. Perhaps, just perhaps, the path you are on will lead to your true destination.

Or imagine you are just beginning your career journey and you have many questions about possible paths and how to get there. You might ask yourself, "What is the right path for me?" "How do I develop the skills to make myself competitive in the marketplace?" "What can I do to ensure success when I do land the right job?"

Or perhaps you want to develop stronger skills in order to advance in your career. Leadership, confidence, goal setting, and adaptability are examples.

In each of these scenarios, a career coach serves as a strong partner in developing a powerful career strategy while empowering the client to choose which career path is right for them. Career coaches are often trainers also and then provide job skills training. Sometimes they serve as counselors on job search strategies, resume development, and interviewing to set clients up for career success whatever their career focus.

This chapter is about staying within the lines and honoring your client and coaching profession by performing the role best suited to what your client wants so that they are moving forward. This chapter outlines the importance of career coaching today, the differences and similarities between a career coach, a counselor, and a trainer, and defines the key core competencies in career coaching. It also explores when to utilize training in career coaching to empower clients.

CAREER COACHING IS IMPORTANT

A 2012 International Coach Federation (ICF) global study found that the coaching industry is approximately a $2 billion dollar industry. Career coaching is proving to be an increasingly popular niche within coaching - and for good reason.

> *"Career coaching is proving to be an increasingly popular niche within coaching - and for good reason."*

According to the U.S. Bureau of Labor Statistics a typical person in their fifties has held an average of 10 jobs during their lifetime. That number is growing. The projected rate for millennial workers (those born 1980-2000) is that they will change jobs every two to four years.

Career coaching helps job seekers navigate the unstable and ever changing job market. It empowers them to discover their strengths, skills, interests, and passions so they make informed decisions about which career path to choose.

> *"Career coaching ... empowers them to discover their strengths, skills, interests, and passions..."*

Career coaching has grown because of the economy's instability. During the most recent economic recession, from the period of 2008-2012, approximately 8.8 million jobs were lost according to the U.S. Bureau of Labor Statistics. Because of this sudden downturn, many employees found themselves back in the job market. Utilizing the resources of a career coach, many were able to develop strategies and find other jobs. Others, without a coach, often pursued a job outside their career because they were anxious to have a job and pay the bills. This of course has long term implications for their opportunities. Once the economy started to improve, many workers sought career coaches to help them transition to jobs that best suited their skills and passions.

In addition to important factors such as the economy playing a large role in the increasing importance of career coaching, many also seek career coaching to realign themselves with their own passions. Gallup conducted a study in 2013 with more than 240,000 workers from over 140 countries and found that only 13% felt they were engaged at work, which means 87% percent of the workers polled indicated they were emotionally disconnected from their workplace.

What is happening? Sometimes, after years in a certain career, individuals feel that something is missing or they are unable to connect their true passions with their work. Other times, people start off in one direction thinking it is the right path for them and then, either through circumstances or a deepening realization of core values, they want a change.

Additionally there are those who seek career coaching to develop skills in order to improve their job performance, develop leadership skills, increase confidence in the work setting, or prepare for promotion.

> *"...seek career coaching to develop skills in order to improve ..."*

Those just starting out in their career seek career coaches to strategize with them on possible career paths, development of job search skills, and help with technical skills such as resume writing, interviewing, and networking to set their best foot forward as they embark on their new journey.

CORE COMPETENCIES

A career coach may also serve in other roles and in order to be aware of what role to play when, following the core competencies outlined by the ICF is an excellent guideline.

While all of the ICF Core Competencies are essential in coaching, the core competencies to additionally highlight in the career coaching role are Meeting Ethical Guidelines and Professional Standards, Establishing the Coaching Agreement, Powerful Questioning, and Creating Awareness.

In order to be successful in the competency of *Meeting Ethical Guidelines and Professional Standards*, the ICF states that the coach "clearly communicates the distinction between coaching, consulting, psychotherapy, and other support professions".

As a career coach, you may perform roles that pertain strictly to coaching and you sometimes also serve in other roles to guide the client, acting as a counselor or trainer. In doing so, you want to make sure the role you are using best supports the client in moving forward and also that the client clearly understands whether you are in the role of a coach, counselor, or trainer. The ICF outlines in its competency rating level chart that someone will not pass the competency of Ethics and Standards if the coach "focuses primarily on telling the client what to do or how to do it."

In the role of a career coach, these lines may be blurred because of the different roles a career coach may perform. For example, when offering certain subject matter expertise, such as helping a client develop a resume or improve interviewing and negotiation skills, this is primarily a training function. In this role, you are providing information on how to perform a certain skill so that they can learn from this skill and utilize it as they move forward in the career process. When performing this role, make it clear to the client you are acting in the role of a trainer and not that of a coach.

Along with the ethical guidelines and professional standards competency, the core competency of *Establishing the Coaching Agreement* is also essential for role clarity. At the start of a coaching relationship, establish an agreement with your client. Part of the agreement encompasses defining boundaries and understanding roles. The ICF outlines some specific guidelines regarding how to excel in this competency. For example, the coach explores what client wants from session, asks the client to establish their measures of success for the session, and ensures clarity about the purpose.

"..the coach explores what client wants …"

In career coaching, it may be tempting to offer training to a client. While training can be useful, be cautious in offering this too quickly. Career coaches first fully explore what will best serve the client by asking probing questions, and then tailor the coaching session to fit what the client wants.

The core competency of *Powerful Questioning* will help in fully engaging the client to explore possibilities and create options. Again, it is all about the client. Career counselors may have some ideas on certain career paths and as a counselor will make suggestions based on assessments. Career coaches use their knowledge and insight to ask powerful questions.

Along with powerful questioning, the competency of *Creating Awareness* will empower the client by fully exploring options and creating possibilities. In order to fulfill this competency, the coach must engage with the client in problem solving instead of using assessments or standardized exercises to determine the solution. A career coach uses the powerful questions to create awareness by having the client find their own answers.

"... create awareness by having the client find their own answers."

ROLE CLARITY: COACH VS. COUNSELOR VS. TRAINER

The term Career Coach may mean different things to different people. Some may mistakenly think of a career coach as

286

someone who administers assessments or gives instruction on career skill development. A Career Coach is someone who supports others through a strategic partnership in helping them achieve career goals. A career coach may perform a number of different roles. What is important as a career coach is understanding what role is being performed and ethically staying within the lines as a coach based on the ICF Code of Ethics and Core Competencies.

To further explore what each of these roles are, let's consider some similarities and differences of a career coach as compared to a career counselor and a trainer.

What is a career counselor? A career counselor can be defined as someone who guides others through career options, career development, and who assists in the career path process. In this process career counselors are likely to use a prescriptive approach by utilizing standardized measures such as assessments to help others with career options. These assessments may help clients with greater self-awareness in areas such as skills, strengths, interests, and personalities. After administering assessments, the counselor guides the client through possible career paths that correspond with results.

While assessments do offer value, there are pros and cons to using them.

On the pro side assessments have the advantage of providing additional information that will help the client determine a particular career path. It gives the client a starting point and a greater awareness of possibilities. For clients struggling to determine a career choice, it helps them narrow the field.

On the con side assessments fail to provide all the answers. For example, missing answers may include understanding one's passions versus skill set and understanding one's interests versus experience and education. Therefore, the career coach wants to be aware of whether and how to use them.

What role do assessments play in coaching versus counseling? Career coaches, if certified with an assessment, also use assessments as a tool for creating awareness and exploring possibilities. What is different between what a career counselor does and what a career coach does is the coaching that comes after debriefing the assessment results. Without follow-up coaching conversations, the client may have limited information to explore their career path possibilities. For example, questions that a career coach explores include: What are their values? What motivates them? What truly interests them? What is their mission statement? What is their long-term vision? By exploring these areas, it is helpful in creating a complete picture and broader understanding for the client.

"What is their mission statement?"

A career counselor's approach is more directive, sometimes offering advice on what to do based on assessment results or what the client has said. Their focus is on providing information, as well as giving answers, and they do so by exploring past experiences and present circumstances. By contrast, a career coach's approach is based on an understanding that the answers are within. They focus on asking the right questions by exploring the client's future goals. They treat the client as their own best expert. In doing so, the coach empowers the client to come up with their own solutions.

Another difference between a career counselor and career coach is the professional relationship between a career counselor and a client tends to be shorter. Once the challenges have been addressed and a plan formulated, the relationship ends. In a coaching relationship, the professional relationship lasts longer. For example, a career coach may work with individuals from the very beginning of career exploration by strategizing which careers to pursue. The career coach is an accountability partner as the client moves forward. Once in a job, a career coach may continue the coaching work with them as the client sets goals for developing professional skills that will move them forward and support being successful in the job. As a client transitions between jobs, a career coach may work with the client in job search strategies, setting goals, and developing an action plan so that the client is exploring their opportunities.

Just as there are similarities and differences between a career coach and a career counselor, the same is also true when comparing a career coach with a trainer. A trainer is primarily a content expert who gives instruction on how to perform or develop specific skills. In doing so, they plan and implement the training and in many cases, set the goals for the outcomes while encouraging the client to achieve those goals.

As discussed previously, career coaching is client-centered. While training is an educational process, coaching is an exploratory process that empowers the client to consider possibilities. Coaches put the client in charge of developing their own goals and solutions. Coaches do, as does the trainer, encourage their client in achieving their goals.

> *"Coaches put the client in charge of developing their own goals and solutions."*

Incorporating training as a career coach can be a very helpful and oftentimes an essential component of career coaching. The point of awareness is that career coaches understand when to coach and when to train, as they are two very different roles. Training and coaching, when used effectively, actually complement each other in career coaching. Key areas of subject matter expertise that a career coach offers clients include job search strategies, resume writing, interviewing, skill development, and salary negotiation.

In any coaching relationship, a coach is to practice client-focused coaching. While a coach may perform similar roles as a career counselor and combine training with coaching, it is very important to understand which role will best empower and move the client forward when, and know how to transition between roles successfully. Following the core competencies outlined by the ICF is an essential component in ensuring that the career coach is indeed staying within the lines.

> *"...it is very important to understand which role will best empower and move the client forward when, and know how to transition between roles successfully."*

To illustrate how a career coach executes various roles with clients, let's meet three individuals in different places where career coaching provides value.

Brad is a 21 year-old college student who is majoring in marketing. He has one more year in college before graduation. He is excited to think about the next phase of his life and starting a new career where he can utilize his knowledge, skills, and strengths. Brad realizes the marketing field is a broad one and is facing challenges narrowing his focus within his chosen field. He knows he is passionate about using his creative talents and is unsure how to align his passions with a career field. Brad is also uncertain how to make himself competitive

291

in the marketplace, and is actively seeking career coaching for job search, resume writing, and interviewing skills.

Because he wants additional direction, Brad utilizes the career coaching services at his university.

Coaching Brad: Brad visits the career coach, Susan, at his university and explains he wishes to explore career options that will leverage his strengths and recent marketing education. He also wants help with job search strategies, resume writing, and interviewing skills. Susan conducts an exploratory conversation with Brad. During this conversation, they discuss the pros and cons of using assessments.

Brad decided he was interested in assessments so Susan explained her process and how she uses them: assessments are one component of the career coaching process used along with coaching to create awareness and explore possibilities with a client. Susan also talked with Brad about training on job search strategies, resume writing, and interviewing. They discussed the difference between this trainer role and the coaching role. Brad decided he wanted to engage in training also. Susan supplied Brad with a written agreement specifically detailing each of these roles and how she was going to use the consulting role with assessments, the trainer role with skill development, and the coaching role to explore and pull it all together.   Because of the conversation and agreement Brad is fully aware of each role and how they will spend their time.

> *"They discussed the difference between this trainer role and the coaching role."*

In the role of the counselor, Susan administered two different assessments.   Upon completion, she debriefed the results with Brad.   In the role of the career coach, Susan spent time with Brad going beyond the surface of the results and digging deeper. She asked him about what most interested him in the occupational areas defined in the results.   She further explored the strengths results by asking Brad to consider what stood out most for him and specifically how he wants to use his strengths in a job position.   Susan joined Brad in the brainstorming process, with Brad's permission, as they explored possible career options.   After the insights gained from the assessments and further exploration with coaching, Brad decided to put together a plan that aligned his strengths with his interests. Susan worked with Brad so he developed action steps to take now and move him toward achieving the plan he developed.

In their next coaching session, Susan asked Brad about his actions steps and how he was moving forward.   He said he felt great about the progress he made and wanted to start developing technical job search skills to help prepare for obtaining a job after graduation.   She asked Brad's permission to take off her coaching hat and put on her training hat so the roles were clearly understood. He gave her permission. She then began to train him regarding skills of how to conduct a job search, write a resume, and interview effectively.

Martha is a 40 year-old project coordinator professional at a global finance company. She has worked 10 years for this company, starting out as an administrative assistant and gradually worked her way up to a project coordinator role. In her current role, she has developed many new skills, taken on higher level responsibilities, and now wants to move into a managerial role.

Martha seeks a career coach to help her develop a strategy and to put a plan in place for facilitating her career growth.

Coaching Martha: When Martha initially begins the conversation with a prospective career coach, she explains she is seeking coaching because she wants to be promoted where she currently works. After the career coach, Stephen, conducts an introductory session and Martha decides the he is a good fit for her, Stephen explains his process. Using this process, he will explore various areas of Martha's life and work with her in establishing goals in these areas.

Martha agrees to this process so the coaching continues.

During the coaching relationship, as Stephen asks probing questions about Martha's work and explores her motivation to move up within the company, Martha begins to realize something. What started as an interest in moving into a managerial role in the company became something completely different. How did she come to this realization?

When Stephen began the coaching process with Martha, he explained the concept of using the whole person approach. In this approach, a coach explores many areas of one's life, such as career, relationships, health, financial, lifestyle, and personal goals. Because Martha engaged in this process, she discovered through the coach's exploratory questions that other goals were more important.

What were the tools Stephen used to help guide Martha through this process?

The opening session with the big picture exploration, and a coaching session with Martha focused on identifying her personal mission statement and core values. After considering many aspects of her life, Martha realized that something was missing in her career. Coming into the coaching process, she thought she wanted additional responsibility and a managerial role, and then she realized the company's culture and values did not align with her own.

Stephen, who was certified in an assessment tool, explained this tool and explored with Martha's using it to add an extra dimension to the coaching process. Martha agreed. The information provided by the assessment, along with deep discussion during the coaching process of exploring the whole person, opened Martha up to new possibilities and created awareness. She realized that her discontent with where she was in her career had more to do with working in a position that did not align with her values and less to do with wanting to move up in the company where she worked.

As Stephen continued probing, Martha realized what she did want. Years before she dreamed of working for a non-profit agency that promoted a healthy environment and sustainable living. She became passionate about this work after doing an internship while she was pursuing a degree in Public Policy. Somewhere along the way, life happened.

After graduation, she had a difficult time finding a job with a non-profit and began working for the global finance company as an Executive Assistant to make ends meet. As she became more involved in the company, she slowly became disconnected from her passion. She felt somewhat dissatisfied in her job. She thought it was due to wanting additional responsibilities. As the coaching continued, she realized it had to do with her wanting to realign herself with her core values, her core passions, and do something that she really felt good about.

The career coach worked with Martha to identify her career goals, aligning them with her skills and passions, and how they fit into other areas of her life. With that, Martha moved forward in pursuing a career in the world of non-profit.

> *"The career coach worked with Martha to identify her career goals, aligning them with her skills and passions, and how they fit into other areas of her life."*

Tom is a 28 year-old local salesperson working for an insurance company. He has been with them for a couple of years and wants to move into a regional sales role. As a regional sales leader, Tom realizes giving group presentations is a requirement and he struggles with confidence. His employer offers a training and development program that incorporates coaching. Tom decides to take the opportunity to work with a coach.

Coaching Tom: Tom wants to be a regional sales manager and recognizes this position requires giving presentations. Tom seeks out his company's internal career coach to build confidence and learn presentation skills.

When Tom meets with the coach, Marcy, he explains what he wants. Marcy checked in with herself to ensure that she had the comfort level to effectively coach Tom and if appropriate, also change roles to provide training using her expertise for presentation skill development. Marcy felt she did have this experience and explained to Tom what she offers. After this discussion, Tom chose to begin the coaching relationship.

Tom told Marcy he wanted to focus on confidence building first. She began to ask powerful questions to create awareness for Tom, including: "Describe a time when you felt confident. How did that make you feel?" "Tell me about a time you overcame a challenge. How did you do it?" "What do you find positive about yourself?" "What do others find positive in you?" "What is holding you back?" "What steps will you take to move you toward what you want?"

Marcy continued to ask probing questions so that Tom was able to bring up memories of times he felt confident, challenges he had overcome, steps he took to overcome them, and verbalize his strengths. In doing so, Tom was able to define the steps he wanted to take now to give him confidence for making presentations.

Marcy also provided a confidence building tool for Tom to use. She took the goals Tom identified and created an affirmation for him to record. Using his words and his goals, Marcy included powerful, positive, and proactive language for Tom. The affirmation supported Tom's focus and motivation to make achieving his goal of moving up as a regional sales manager a reality. He actually saw and heard himself giving spectacular presentations and feeling confident as he spoke.

As Tom's confidence grew, he focused on becoming more proficient in creating visual presentations and developing his own unique delivery style. Tom shared his lack of knowledge. Because Marcy had experience in this area, she asked permission to take off her coaching hat and put on her training hat in order to give Tom some presentation skill training. Tom agreed and Marcy had several sessions with him focused on presentation development. Throughout this process, she also coached Tom on creating action steps and provided accountability as they continued to meet.

The career coach supported Tom as he built his confidence, developed his skills, and advanced his career.

In each of these roles, the career coach had the conversation with the client about what they wanted, was very clear in terms of their role as a coach, trainer, or counselor, when they performed each, and utilized training and assessments as a complement to the coaching process.

"...the career coach ... was very clear in terms of their role as a coach, trainer, or counselor, when they performed each..."

APPLICATION OF INSIGHTS

Career coaches have a variety of tools in their toolkit. Depending on the situation or where a client is in the process, a career coach may implement other roles: training - teaching a client a certain skill or technique, and counseling - providing assessments as a supplement to the coaching conversation. With each of these implementations, the career coach works with a client on their goals, action planning, and timelines. The skillful career coach knows when to perform each role.

The key points for consideration are:

- Understand which role will best serve the client and when.
- Ensure the client knows which role you are performing.
- Use assessments only if you are certified, only when appropriate, and follow it up with the coaching process.
- Be knowledgeable and up to date on skills that will help your client and incorporate training as appropriate.
- Transparently combine coaching with training or counseling as you move your client forward.

Effective career coaching empowers clients with exploration of knowledge, interests, and motivating factors. Career coaching helps clients develop skills to enhance opportunities and move them toward goals. Career coaching creates confidence, inspiring the client to live a passionate and fulfilling life.

300

Amy Gamblin is a Certified Master Coach and Certified Coach Trainer with the Center for Coaching Certification. She is founder of SpotOn Business Services specializing in career coaching along with personal and professional development workshops for universities.

Amy's mission is to empower, inspire, and motivate others through strategic and focused collaboration. She is making a difference individually and throughout communities offering encouragement and fostering growth for success.

Amy has over 15 years experience with a background in project management and training. She has implemented global training procedures, served as lead coordinator on multi-million dollar projects, and developed best practices and standard operating procedures for international teams. She is experienced in strategic planning, research and analysis, and training and development.

Amy holds a Bachelor of Arts in History from the University of Kentucky and Master of Arts in Diplomacy and International Relations from the Patterson School of Diplomacy. She is a member of the International Coach Federation, Professional Association of Resume Writers, and National Career Development Association.